The Spielberger German Armor
& Military Vehicles Series
Vol.IV

Walter J. Spielberger

Panzer IV

& Its Variants

Schiffer Military/Aviation History
Atglen, PA

Cover and jacket: Siegfried Horn

Photo sources: Federal Archives/Military Archives (13), P. Chamberlain collection (6), Hilary Doyle collection (5), Uwe Feist archives (22), Tom Jentz collection (1), Robert J. Icks collection (10), Ingo Kasten archives (19), Charles J. Kliment collection (1), Werner Oswald archives (1), Panssarimuseo Finland (1), Graf Seherr-Thoss (9), Shrivenham Museum (4), Walter J. Spielberger archives (208), F. Wiener collection (3).

Scale drawings by Hilary H. Doyle.
Color illustrations by Uwe Feist.
Technical editing by Tom Jentz.

Translated from the German by Edward Force.

Copyright © 1993 by Schiffer Publishing Ltd.
Library of Congress Catalog Number: 93-84495

Printed in China
ISBN: 0-88740-515-0

This book was originally published under the title,
Der Panzerkampfwagen IV und seine Abarten,
by Motorbuch Verlag, Stuttgart

We are interested in hearing from authors with book ideas on related topics.

Published by Schiffer Publishing Ltd.
4880 Lower Valley Road
Atglen, PA 19310
Phone: (610) 593-1777; Fax: (610) 593-2002 E-mail: Info@schifferbooks.com
Please visit our web site catalog at www.schifferbooks.com

We are always looking for people to write books on new and related subjects.
If you have an idea for a book, please contact us at the above address.
This book may be purchased from the publisher.
Include $3.95 for shipping. Please try your bookstore first.
You may write for a free catalog.

In Europe, Schiffer books are distributed by:
Bushwood Books
6 Marksbury Ave.
Kew Gardens
Surrey TW9 4JF
England
Phone: 44 (0)208 392-8585 Fax: 44 (0)208 392-9876
E-mail: Info@bushwoodbooks.co.uk
Website: www.bushwoodbooks.co.uk
Free postage in the UK. Europe: air mail at cost.

CONTENTS

Foreword **8**

B.W. Prototype (Rh) – Rheinmetall **10**

B.W. Prototype (K) – Krupp **12**

Design VK 2002 (MAN) – MAN **12**

Panzerkampfwagen IV (75mm) Ausf. A, 1/BW – Krupp-Gruson **13**

Panzerkampfwagen IV (75mm) Ausf. B, 2/BW – Krupp-Gruson **28**

Panzerkampfwagen IV (75mm) Ausf. C, 3/BW – Krupp-Gruson **29**

Panzerkampfwagen IV (75mm) Ausf. D, 4/ & 5/BW – Krupp-Gruson **32**

Panzerkampfwagen IV (75mm) Ausf. E, 6/BW – Krupp-Gruson **34**

Panzerkampfwagen IV (75mm) (Tauch), BW – Krupp-Gruson, Alkett **39**

Panzerkampfwagen IV (75mm) Ausf. F1, 7/BW – Krupp, Vomag, Ni-Werke **40**

Panzerkampfwagen IV with 50mm KwK 39 L/60 – Prototype – Krupp, Ni-Werke **48**

Panzerkampfwagen IV (75mm L/43) Ausf. F2, 7/BW – Krupp, Vomag, Ni-Werke **50**

Panzerkampfwagen IV (Tp), BW – Krupp-Gruson **50**

Panzerkampfwagen IV with Snowplow, BW – various **50**

Panzerkampfwagen IV (75mm L/43) Ausf. G, 7/BW – Krupp, Vomag, Ni-Werke **54**

Panzerkampfwagen IV with Sloped Armor, Proposal – Krupp-Gruson **59**

Panzerkampfwagen IV (75mm L/48) Ausf. H, BW – Krupp, Vomag, Ni-Werke **63**

Panzerbefehlswagen IV, BW – various **66**

Panzerbeobachtungswagen IV, BW – various **66**

Panzerkampfwagen IV (75mm L/48) Ausf. J, BW – Ni-Werke **68**

Road Plow on Panzer IV Chassis, BW – various **72**

Panzerkampfwagen IV – Dummy – Lohner **73**

Panzerkampfwagen IV with Hydrostatic Drive, Prototype –Zahnradfabrik
    Augsburg **73**

Panzerkampfwagen VK 3001 – Prototype – Daimler-Benz **76**

Panzerkampfwagen VK 3001 – Prototype – Henschel **76**

Panzerkampfwagen VK 3001 – Prototype – MAN **76**

Panzerkampfwagen VK 3001 – Prototype – Porsche **76**

Panzerkampfwagen IV with Panther Turret, Proposal – Krupp-Gruson **78**

Panzerkampfwagen IV Ausf. X – Gerät 551 **80**

Panzerkampfwagen IV with Independent Suspension – Prototype –Krupp-Gruson **80**

105mm K 18 auf Panzer-Selbstfahrlafette IVa – Krupp-Gruson **87**

Sturmgeschütz (new) – Proposal – Alkett **88**

Sturmgeschütz 43 auf Panzer IV Chassis (Gerät 822) **89**

Sturmhaubitze 43 auf Panzer IV Chassis (Gerät 823) **89**

Sturmgeschütz with Panzer III, IV and Leopard Components –Proposal **89**

Leichte Panzerjäger auf Panzer IV Chassis with Rounded Front –Vomag **92**

Jagdpanzer IV, Ausf. F – Vomag **92**

Panzerjäger IVb (E 39) – Krupp-Gruson **92**

Jagdpanzer IV with Rigid Mounted Gun **95**

Sturmgeschütz auf Einheitsfahrgestell III/IV with 75mm L/70 **96**

Panzer IV/70 (A) – Ni-Werke **97**

Panzer IV/70 (V) – Vomag **99**

Panzerjäger IV with 88mm Pak 43/3, Proposal – Krupp **100**

Panzerkampfwagen IV with Recoilless 75mm Antitank Gun, Proposal –Krupp **100**

21 bzw. 22 cm Mörser auf Panzer IV Fahrgestell, Proposal **101**

Sturmpanzerwagen 604/16 (Gerät 581), Proposal – Alkett **101**

Sturmpanzer IV, Pre-series – HZA Vienna, Saurer, Graz-Simmering-Pauker **102**

Sturmpanzer IV, First Series – DEW **105**

Sturmpanzer IV, Final Series – DEW **105**

38 cm Wurfgerät auf Panzer IV – Proposal **105**

30.5 cm Mörser M.16 auf Panzer IV Fahrgestell (Gerät 565), Proposal **105**

Carrier 604/14 for 30.5 cm Mortar on Panzer III/IV Chassis, Proposal – Skoda **105**

Selbstfahrlafette Flak IV (20mm Flakvierling), Prototype – BMM **106**

Selbstfahrlafette Flak IV (37mm Flak) – DEW **109**

Flakpanzer IV with 37mm Doppelflak 43, Prototype – Alkett **114**

30mm Doppelflak Brünn or Rheinmetall in U-Boat Turret on Panzer IV Chassis,
    Design **114**

Flakpanzer IV (20mm) auf Panzer IV/3 "Wirbelwind" – Ostbau **115**

Leichter Flakpanzer mit 37mm Flak 43 auf Panzer IV Ausf. J "Ostwind" – DEW **115**

Flakpanzer "Ostwind II" mit 37mm Flakzwilling 44, Prototype –Ostbau **116**

Leichter Flakpanzer IV (30mm) "Kugelblitz" – Daimler-Benz **117**

Geschützwagen III/IV (Gerät 804) für leFH 18/40/2 (Sf), Prototype – Alkett **122**

Geschützwagen III/IV (Gerät 807) für sFH 18/1 (Sf), Prototype – Alkett **122**

Geschützwagen III/IV (Gerät 812) for sFH 18/5 (Sf), Prototype – Alkett **122**

88mm Pak 43/1 auf Panzer III/IV Fahrgestell (Sf) – DEW **122**

s.Pz. Haubitze 18/1 auf Panzer III/IV Fahrgestell (Sf) – DEW **122**

Munitionsträger "Hummel" – DEW **128**

leFH 18/40 with All-round Fire on Gw III/IV, removable onto cruciform mount,
    Proposal **128**

88mm Pak 48 on leFH Self-Propelled Chassis. Proposal –Rheinmetall, Krupp **128**

12.8 Gun on leFH Self-Propelled Chassis, Proposal **128**

Self-Propelled leFH with Leopard Components **128**

Self-Propelled leFH with Sturmgeschütz (new) Components **129**

Self-Propelled leFH with 105mm leFH 43 "Heuschrecke", Prototype –Krupp **131**

Self-Propelled leFH with 105mm leFH 43, Prototype – Rheinmetall, Daimler-Benz **132**

leFH with cruciform mount similar to Flak Gun, Proposal – Krupp **132** leFH 18/1 (Sf), Geschützwagen IVb – Krupp **132**

"Hummel-Wespe" Vehicle as Universal Self-Propelled Artillery Carriage,
    Proposal **132**

Mittlerer Waffenträger mit 150mm sFH 18, Proposal **134**

Mittlerer Waffenträger mit 128mm K 81, Proposal **134**

Brückenleger Panzer IV, Test Chassis, Prototype – Krupp **135**

Brückenleger Panzer IV, Production Chassis, Prototype – Krupp **135**

Brückenleger Panzer IV, Production Chassis, Prototype – Magirus **135**

Infanterie Sturmsteg auf Panzer IV, Prototype – Magirus **141**

Panzerkampfwagen IV Ausf. F, Munitionsträger für Karlgerät –Krupp **141**

Panzerfähre, Prototype – Magirus **143**

Panzerkampfwagen IV Fahrgestell for Sturmgeschütz Tests, Prototype – Krupp **143**

Bergepanzer IV – various **143**

Foreword

This volume of the "Military Vehicles" Series is an attempt to portray the technical development of the German Wehrmacht's most important battle tank. Originally conceived merely as a support vehicle, the Panzer IV nevertheless formed the backbone of the German Panzer units during the war years through timely modifications.

How little the concept of using the Panzer IV in the East European arena had been considered in forming its basic concept became very clear after the events of June 1941. Stringent weight limits that allowed strengthening the armor to only a limited degree, insufficient cross-country maneuverability because of excessively high ground pressure, and the modest engine power constantly set limits to the modernization of the original design. However, it was possible, as with the Panzer III, to utilize makeshift solutions to suit the quickly changing conditions. In terms of weaponry, after the installation of the long tank gun, all enemy tanks could be fought successfully.

Since this vehicle was one of the few combat vehicles of the German Army to be produced in really large series throughout the war years, it was also utilized for an almost endless list of special purposes. Defining these was part of our task here.

When one examines this development, one sees Hitler's personal influence running through the whole of German tank development. It affected not only individual details of tank design, but also decisively influenced, through constant intervention, the course of production.

In addition, the problem of insufficient supplies of raw materials made itself felt again and again, making any large-scale expansion of production impossible. Problems in the creation of tank-manufacturing facilities as well as the production of machine tools caused further difficulties in the tank production program.

It can be seen clearly today how far apart the concepts of military planners and the potentialities of industry were, for industry was simply not in any condition to provide adequate supplies for the troops.

What was actually accomplished could only rely on available technology, is a basic historical fact. The very numerous changes and interventions led to a fragmentation of the already limited production and made tanks become truly rare pieces of equipment in the German Wehrmacht. It was the troops in particular who came to feel this shortage again and again.

In spite of this, the Panzer IV played a significant role in the motorization of the German Army.

As usual, important documents and details of these vehicles are lacking, and it is always surprising to see how much material could be assembled through painstaking attention to small details. Almost no materials on the first stages of Panzer IV development have been found to date. The fact that we seem to have presented an almost complete history nevertheless is a tribute above all to the tireless interest of Hilary L. Doyle and Tom L. Jentz. After my archives were destroyed, Col. Robert J. Icks provided the basis for their reconstruction. Dr. Fritz Wiener also contributed a considerable share. For the revision of the Flakpanzer chapter and a large part of the photographic material used in it, I extend hearty thanks to Graf Seherr-Thoss, who provided the decisive contribution to this development. Where original drawings could no longer be found, the excellent research of the British School of Tank Technology was relied on to contribute some of the best material in this area.

In addition, I wish to thank Mr. P. Chamberlain, Uwe Feist and H. Scultetus for their years of cooperation.

Walter J. Spielberger, 1977

The Panzerkampfwagen IV & its Variants

The concept that led the way to the development of future German tanks had already been formulated in detail by the work group gathered around, the later Generaloberst, Heinz Guderian in 1930. At that time no one could imagine that this tank, conceived at that time as only a support vehicle, would accompany the German armored troops from the height of their success to the depths of their defeat.

In 1930 two basic types of tanks were advocated as the final equipment of the Panzer troops, these being a tank with an armor-piercing weapon plus a support vehicle with a large-caliber gun.

For the vehicles of the 18-ton class, the support tanks, the disguised name of "Begleitwagen" (BW) was established. The names of these armored and artillery developments forbidden by the Treaty of Versailles continued to evolve from 1935.

The last outstanding questions as to the armored equipment for the Reichsheer, which was to be expanded to 63 divisions, were dealt with for the most part on January 11, 1934.

The "BW" vehicle was to equip the medium companies, the support companies of the planned Panzer units. The armament of these vehicles with a large-caliber tank gun and with two machine guns, one in the turret and one in the bow, would make it possible for them to hold their own in battle against light tanks and attack targets for which the lighter armor-piercing weapon of the "ZW" vehicle was not suitable. Therefore a gun caliber of 75mm was decided on. An early designation for this medium tank was the "Gesch.Kpfw. (75mm) (Vskfz. 618)" which was officially changed on April 3, 1936 to the "Panzerkampfwagen IV (7,5 cm) (Vskfz.622.).''

The firm of Rheinmetall was already taking part, in competition with the Krupp firm, in the development of an 18-ton vehicle as of 1930. An experimental vehicle was completed by Rheinmetall, but after certain changes, some of which were based on features of the Rheinmetall-Borsig vehicle, the Krupp version was chosen for production.

One of the first prototypes of the "BW" vehicle built by Rheinmetall beginning in 1930; side, front and rear views.

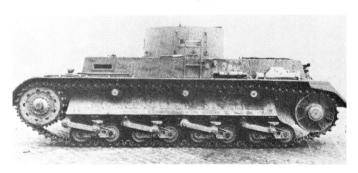

The wooden model of the Rheinmetall proposal for the "BW" vehicle.

The Rheinmetall prototype had Wilson steering gears with frontal drive. It was to be armed with a 75mm tank gun as well as two machine guns. The weight of the vehicle was 18 tons, and the motor was to produce 300 horsepower. A top speed of 35 km/hr was to be reached. All of the duties were divided among a five-man crew. The strength of the armor varied, with the front plates 16 to 20 mm thick, while 13 mm side armor was planned. So was radio equipment. The running gear designed by the Rheinmetall firm featured eight small double-mounted road wheels and three return rollers on each side. The long suspension arms, were similar to those of the "Neubaufahrzeuge" designed by Rheinmetall. The design for the adjustable idler wheel mount was changed several times.

Another prototype vehicle by Rheinmetall featured modified suspension. The exhaust system was also modified.

The Krupp firm already had a prototype for the "ZW" vehicle in the works at that time. This photograph shows the "M.K.A." export tank, the body of which shows a certain similarity to the first Panzer IV.

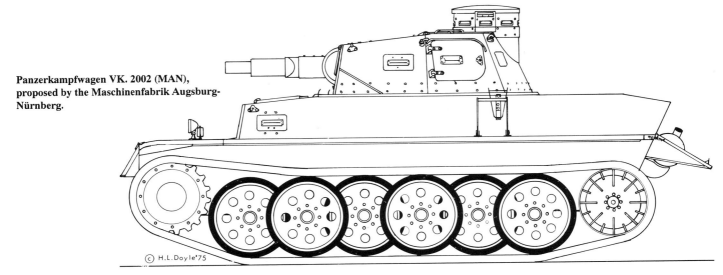

Panzerkampfwagen VK. 2002 (MAN),
proposed by the Maschinenfabrik Augsburg-
Nürnberg.

The Krupp firm's design adhered strictly to the technical requirements that had then been set for the "BW" vehicles. The overall weight was set at 18 tons, with an engine performance of 320 horsepower. The top speed was to be 30 km/hr. With exterior dimensions of 5600 x 2900 x 2650 mm and plate thicknesses of 5 to 14.5 mm, a climbing ability of 30 degrees was required. Trenches up to 2.2 meters in width could be crossed. 140 rounds for the primary weapon and 3000 rounds for the machine guns were to be carried.

The wooden mockup of the Krupp proposal for the "BW" vehicle. The weapon installation is similar to that of the first Panzer III tanks. The front wall is straight. Beside it is a wooden mockup of the "Neubaufahrzeug."

According to the practices of the Heeres Waffenamt [Army Ordnance Department], in due time other manufacturers were also invited to offer suggestions for a medium tank. In addition to a VK. 2001 (K) from Krupp AG, the Maschinenfabrik Augsburg-Nürnberg AG [MAN] offered a design for a VK 2002 (MAN). Both versions featured the interleaved suspension already influenced by E. Kniepkamp, but this was not considered for the production vehicle. The hull, armored superstructure and turret already showed a certain similarity with the later production model. With its design for the "BW" turret, the Heerlein Department of the Fried.Krupp AG essentially assumed the responsibility for all further turret designs. With few exceptions (notably the Panther), Krupp maintained a virtual monopoly in turret design until the end of the war.

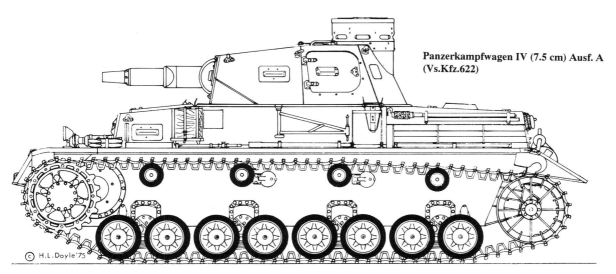

Panzerkampfwagen IV (7.5 cm) Ausf. A
(Vs.Kfz.622)

© H.L.Doyle'75

After evaluating the design proposed by Krupp, the first prototypes were built, to be ready for testing in 1935-36. On the basis of testing experiences the Heeres Waffenamt selected the firm of Fried.Krupp AG as the final developmental and production firm for the entire vehicle. The "O-Serie" was still built in Essen, while series production of the "BW" vehicles began in October of 1937 at the Krupp-Grusonwerk in Magdeburg-Buckau.

The 35 Panzerkampfwagen Ausf. A, with the type designation "1/BW", were delivered by mid 1938. Their chassis number series ran from 80101 to 80135. The fighting weight, with armor basis of 14,5 mm, amounted to 17.3 tons. The vehicles were recognizable externally by the projecting driver's compartment and the barrel-shaped commander's cupola without external visors. An MG 34 machine gun was positioned in a ball mount in front of the radio operator. 122 rounds were carried for the 75mm tank gun plus 3000 rounds of ammunition for the two MG 34's.

The tank consisted of the chassis, the armored superstructure attached on top of it, and the turret. The armored hull functioned as the chassis. It consisted of the closed bow section, the open central hull, and the open rear section, which were constructed of several armor plates of varying thicknesses welded together. The sidewalls were mutually reinforced by transverse members. Likewise the rear wall was reinforced to carry the adjustable idler wheel axles. The engine and drive train were mounted in the armored hull. The engine, a 12-cylinder Maybach "HL 108 TR" with twin carburetors, was housed in the rear section of the hull.

The engine cooling system was driven by double V-belts from pulleys on the engine crankshaft to the drivegear for the twin fans. The cooling system was designed to provide sufficient cooling at temperatures up to +30 degrees celsius.

The first trial vehicle of the "BW" series under construction by Krupp. The running gear is not yet complete. The step-shaped driver's compartment is easy to see. On the right side, above the spade, is the wooden protective bar for the antenna. Designation: "Geschützkampfwagen (7.5 cm) (Vs.Kfz. 618, later 622)."

Upper left: the right side with various equipment.

Above: The divided entry hatch for the driver and radio operator is typical of the first production version. The weapon installation with inner gun mantle is also easy to see.

The first type of commander's cupola was set into the rear turret wall. The details of the driver's visor can also be seen.

This drawing shows the drive train from the rear engine through the transmission via steering gears to the front drive wheels.

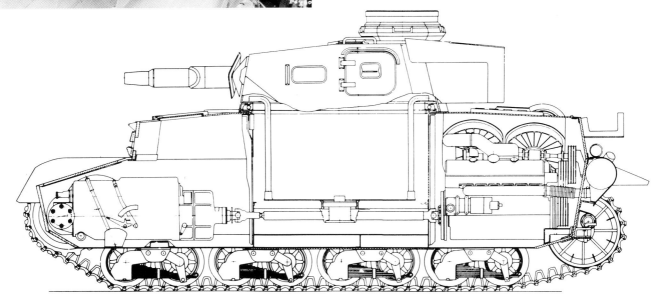

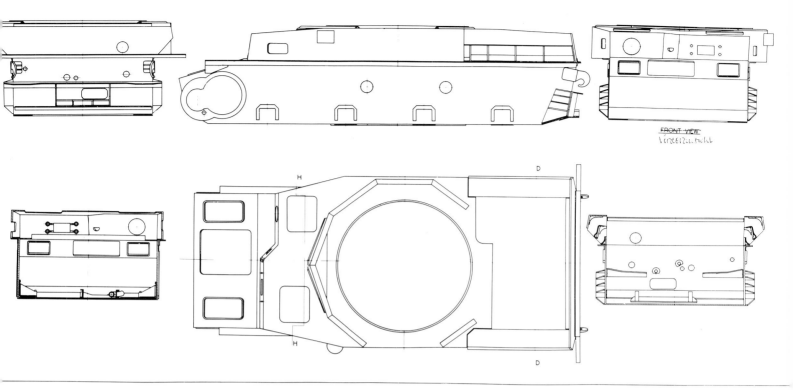

FRONT VIEW
Vorderansicht

Details of the hull of Panzerkampfwagen IV, Ausf. D.

Longitudinal and transverse drawings of the hull and superstructure. The latter was designed to be removable.

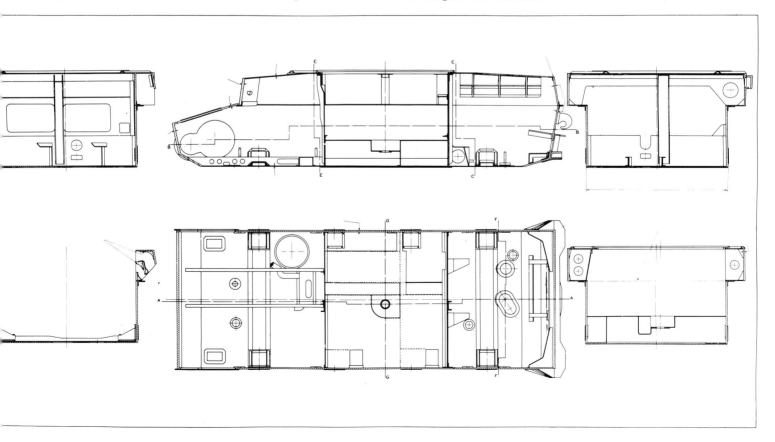

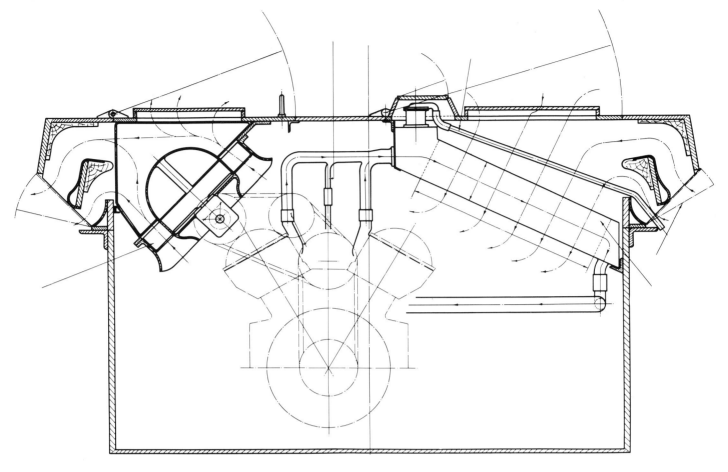

The engine compartment, showing the entry and exhaust ducts for cooling air.

The exhaust fans, driven by a belt from the engine.

Housed below the fighting compartment were three fuel tanks with a total capacity of 453 liters. A valve could be set to allow any individual tank to be used until it ran dry.

A firewall with openings for the power train, rods and electric lines divided the engine compartment from the fighting compartment.

A door in this firewall afforded access to the engine area from the fighting compartment. The driveshaft ran from the engine through the fighting compartment in a tunnel to the bow area, via a dry three-plate clutch to the five-speed ZF "Allklauen SFG 75" transmission. The bevel gears and the steering mechanism were flanged at the front of the transmission. The clutch-type steering mechanism

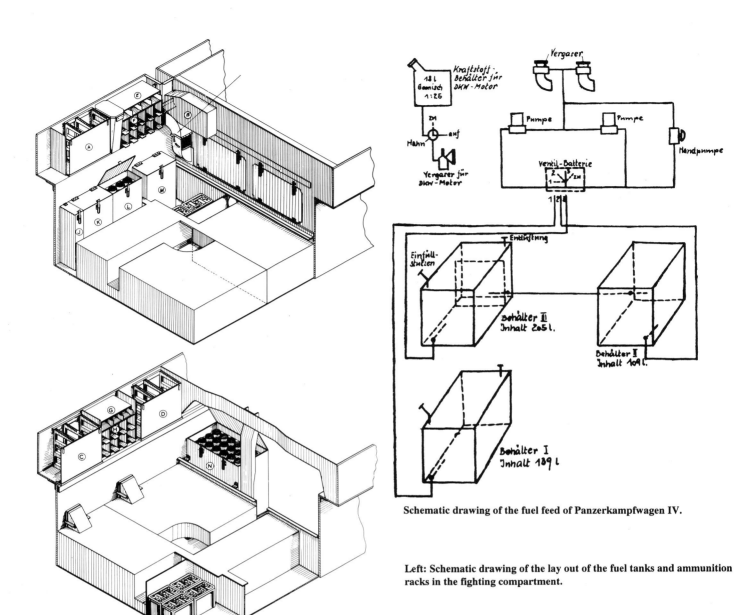

Schematic drawing of the fuel feed of Panzerkampfwagen IV.

Left: Schematic drawing of the lay out of the fuel tanks and ammunition racks in the fighting compartment.

was a Wilson design produced by Krupp. From the steering mechanism, two driveshafts ran left and right to the two steering brakes and the two final drives. The steering brakes inside, the final drives with the drive wheels outside, were attached to the sidewalls of the hull.

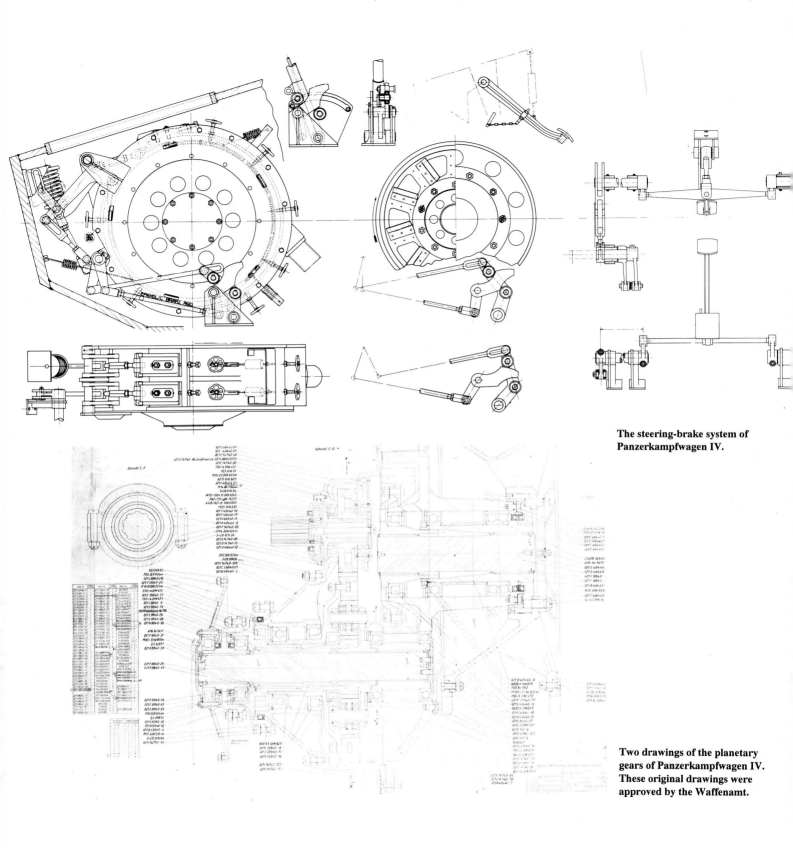

The steering-brake system of
Panzerkampfwagen IV.

Two drawings of the planetary
gears of Panzerkampfwagen IV.
These original drawings were
approved by the Waffenamt.

Right, top to bottom: The suspension for the Panzer IV (external drawing).

Drawing from above, showing the road wheel bogie assembly.

The road wheel bogie assembly, seen from underneath.

Next to the transmission were the driver's seat on the left and the radio operator's seat on the right.

Between the drive wheel and the idler wheel on each side were four bogie assemblies, each with two 470 x 75-660 road wheels suspended on longitudinal quarter-elliptic springs. The distance between axles on each bogie assembly was 500 mm.

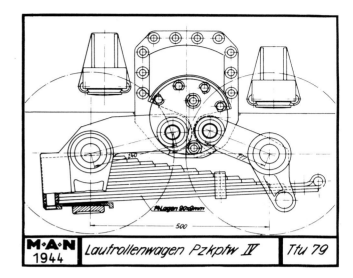

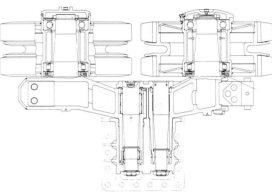

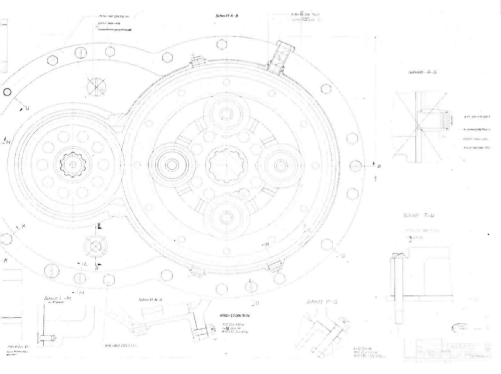

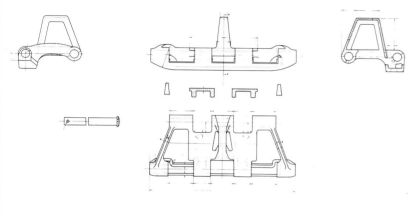

Above: The track links of Panzer IV, with pins removed and installed.

Left: Details of a track link, longitudinal and transverse views.

Lower left: Track link grouser for the Panzer III and IV. 1. Grouser installed, 2. Splint, 3. Track link, 4. Splint, 5. Grouser.

Lower right: Snow grousers, used on Panzer III and IV.

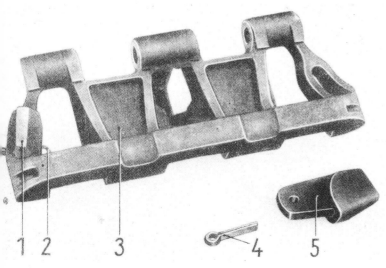

1 2 3 4 5

The upper length of the track was carried and guided by four 250 x 65-135 return rollers. The tracks, their links having a width of 360 mm, were guided over all the wheels. The links were attached to each other by pins. The track length on the ground was 3.72 meters. Track grousers were later available for use on ice and packed snow in the winter.

Protection above the running gear was provided by sheet-metal fenders. The bottom of the hull was protected by a large armor plate beneath the fuel tanks. There were ten openings in the hull bottom for maintenance access. Under the radio operator's seat was a round escape hatch through which the crew could dismount while under fire.

The superstructure of the Panzerkampfwagen IV consisted of the upper part of the armored body and the turret. The superstructure was designed for a five-man crew. The superstructure protected the fighting compartment and part of the driver's and radio operator's positions. It consisted of the front wall, the left and right sidewalls, the roof and the rear wall that separated the fighting compartment from the engine compartment. The frontal armor was reinforced inside by cross members, steps and braces. The superstructure sides extended out over the hull of the vehicle. The space thus gained served for ammunition and equipment storage.

Vision ports had been cut in the front wall and the forward sidewalls. The driver's vision port was covered by a visor. Two hatches were located in the superstructure roof above the driver and radio operator positions. In the Ausf. A the hatch covers were made in two pieces, but subsequent models were fitted with one-piece hatch covers.

In the left sidewall there was a ventilator opening for the steering brakes, with a cap to protect it from shot damage. At the left rear of the roof was a fuel-filler opening for the DKW engine in the auxiliary generator set.

A circular opening was cut into the superstructure roof to carry the turret ring, 1680 mm in diameter, that held the ball bearings for the turret race. The gap between the turret and the superstructure was covered by angular protective shot deflectors.

The radio operator's seat, showing a. the MG 34 installed in the ball mount, b. the radio modulator, c. the receiver modulator, f. the radio operator's gas mask, and g. two spare belts for the machine gun. The radio equipment is at the radio operator's left.

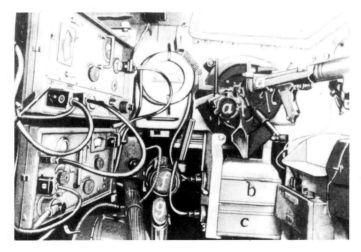

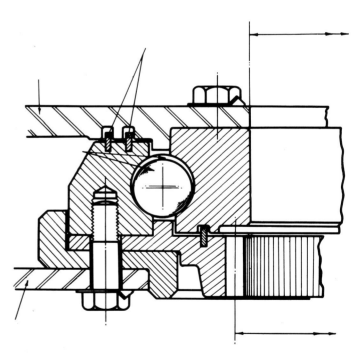

Drawing of the turret ring, showing the ball bearing race.

On the right superstructure sidewall, a wooden rail was mounted to protect the antenna and for storage of the spare antenna rod. Under the wooden rail was the holder for a spade.

In the inside of the superstructure, on the right sidewall, was a brace with a flange for the antenna to pass through. Under the driver's visor, blue warning lights were mounted. These warning lights switched on warning the driver when the barrel of the 75mm KwK gun was traversed beyond the profile of the vehicle. Inside, on the superstructure roof between the driver and radio operator, hung a frame for mounting the radio transmitter and receiver. The navigational gyrocompass was also inside, at the left front corner of superstructure.

The rear deck protected the engine compartment. The intake for the engine-cooling air was located on the left side and the cooling-air exhaust on the right side. In the roof of the rear deck were the radiator hatch, the engine hatch and the ventilator fan hatch. Inside was the mounting that held the radiators in place. Under the ventilator fan hatch hung the framework that held both of the engine cooling fans.

On the right side of the Panzerkampfwagen IV a two-meter-long rod antenna was mounted, which could be lowered into a protective wooden carrier. Raising and lowering the antenna was done from inside the vehicle. The antenna was a hollow rod of thin hard copper sheet (Cuprodur).

The turret mounted on a ball bearing race could be traversed through 360 degrees. The turret ring had 324 teeth on its inside surface, and was attached by its outer flange, along with the fixed outer ball-bearing race, to a ring riveted onto the upper armor plate. Traversing gears engaged the teeth on the turret ring.

The turret front plate was at an angle of 80 degrees, the other walls at 65 degrees to the horizontal plane. In the turret front plate were two observation ports, one on either side of the gun mantle. The turret was closed off at the top by its roof, with the commander's cupola fastened to the rear. There was one entry hatch and one vision port cut into each side of the turret. The entry hatches were covered by one-piece hatch covers, the vision ports by visors.

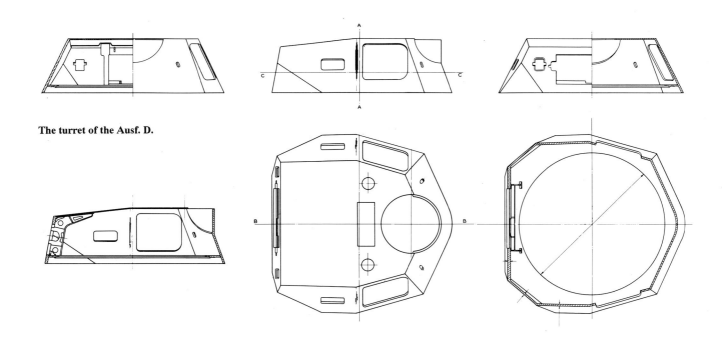

The turret of the Ausf. D.

The gun mantle held the gun cradle with the 7.5 cm gun, recoil cylinder and pneumatic recuperator, as well as a mount for the MG 34 machine gun. The internal gun mantle was made of curved armor plate closed off at each end by sidewalls that held the trunnions. A wall was set into the rear to which the gun cradle and the machine-gun mount were attached. An external mantle, fastened to the turret front plates, covered the spaces around the internal gun mantle.

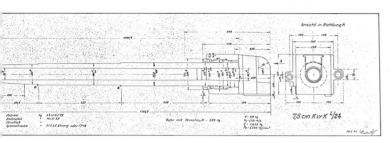

Longitudinal drawing of the primary weapon.

The 7.5 cm KwK L/24 tank gun.

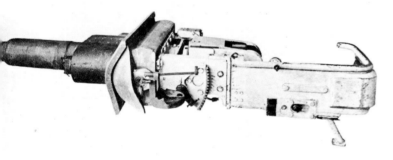

The tank gun consisted of the gun barrel with its breech, the gun cradle with the recoil cylinder and pneumatic recuperator, the electric firing circuit plus equipment and parts. The turret machine gun was installed in a mount with an adjusting apparatus. The "Turmzielfernrohr 5" telescopic gun sight was built into the gun mantle and its rear support was fastened to the turret roof. A "7.5 cm und MG 34" open gun sight could be used to aim the guns if the telescopic sight was put out of action.

The gun was aimed by mechanical elevation gear and by traversing the turret either by hand or with the electric motor. Under normal conditions the turret was traversed using the electric motor mounted vertically under the elevation mechanism on the turret race. A voltage regulated motor controller was used to govern the traverse speed. Electric power was supplied by the auxiliary generator set. The gasoline-electric auxiliary generator set mounted in the engine compartment consisted of a DKW

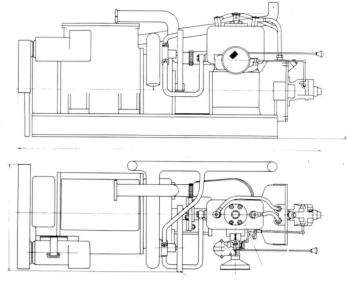

Schematic drawing of the auxiliary generator set.

two-cylinder engine and the electric generator.

By September 30, 1939, 211 Panzerkampfwagen IV (Vs.Kfz.622) had been manufactured.

Upper left: Mounted on the left side of the tank were: a. Wooden block for winch, b. Fire extinguisher, c. Two S-shaped towing hooks, d. Large wire cutters, e. Track adjusting wrench, f. Track spanner, g. Wrecking bars (1 long, 1 short), h. Gun cleaning rods with cover.

Left center: Mounted on the right side were: a. Steel cable (on rear), b. 5 smoke cartridges, c. Two wrenches for track-tensioner nuts, d. 4 track links, e. Starter crank, f. Long-handled spade, g. Jack, h. Medium axe, i. Tool box.

Left page, right: Inside the fighting compartment: a. Flare pistol, b. Box of 12 flare cartridges, c. 19 MG 34 ammunition drums and 24 7.5 cm rounds, d. Commander's and loader's packs, e. MG 34 standard mount for anti-aircraft use, f. Gunner's pack.

The two photographs below show Panzerkampfwagen IV in its intended role as a support tank for the lighter Panzerkampfwagen I and II.

Above: The five-man crew of a Panzer IV. Inside in front are the driver and radio operator, at right in the turret the loader, opposite the gunner, in the center the commander.

Panzerkampfwagen IV Ausf. B to E, were produced using the following Fgst.Nr. [chassis number] series:

Ausf. B   (2/BW) Fgst.Nr. 80201 - 80300
Ausf. C   (3/BW) Fgst.Nr. 80301 - 80500
Ausf. D   (4/BW) Fgst.Nr. 80501 - 80700
Ausf. D   (5/BW) Fgst.Nr. 80701 - 80748
Ausf. E   (6/BW) Fgst.Nr. 80801 - 81500

For the individual models, the following thicknesses (in mm) of armor plate were used:

Ausf.	Hull Front	Hull Sides	Hull Bottom	Gun Mantle	Turret Front	Turret Sides
B	30	14.5	5	30	30	14.5
C	30	14.5	5	30	30	14.5
D	30	20	10	35	30	20
E	50	20	20	10	35	30

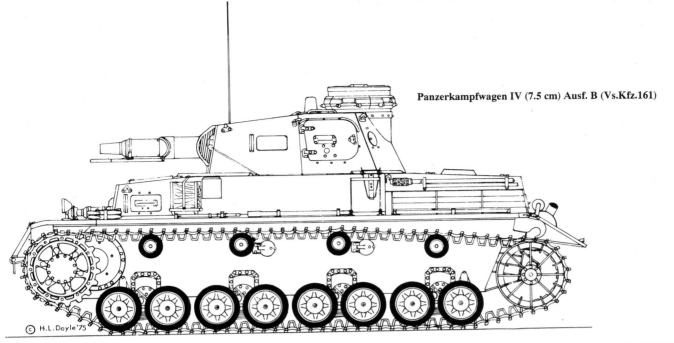

Panzerkampfwagen IV (7.5 cm) Ausf. B (Vs.Kfz.161)

© H.L.Doyle '75

Upper left: Panzerkampfwagen IV, Ausf. A, in use during the occupation of the Sudetenland. Vehicle parade in Komotau on October 9, 1938.

Right: The second production version of Panzerkampfwagen IV had a modified superstructure with the front armor plate in one plane. This photograph shows a wooden dummy before the start of production.

Lower left: These vehicles received their baptism of fire in Poland in 1939.

The first and second production versions of Panzerkampfwagen IV side by side. Vehicles of the 3rd Panzer Regiment in Brno on March 22, 1939.

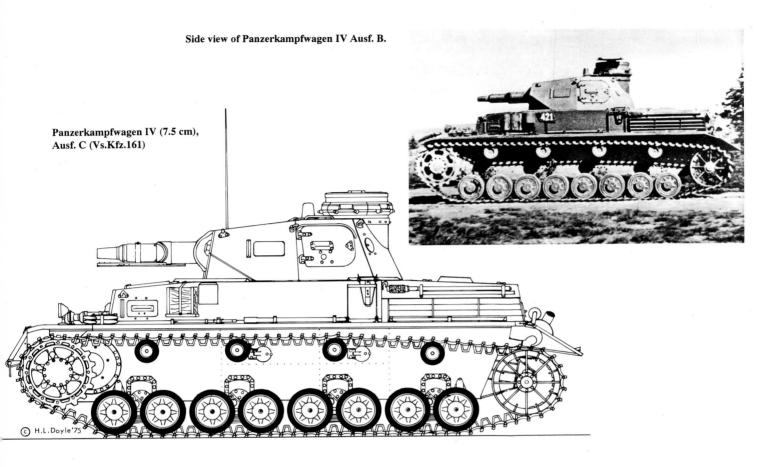

Side view of Panzerkampfwagen IV Ausf. B.

Panzerkampfwagen IV (7.5 cm),
Ausf. C (Vs.Kfz.161)

© H.L.Doyle '75

The Panzerkampfwagen IV Ausf. C appeared in 1938 and was almost identical to the previous model. The MG 34 next to the tank gun was now protected by a cylindrical armor shield.

As with the Ausf.A, the Ausf. B through E were armed with a short 7.5 cm tank gun and an MG 34 in the turret. In addition, an MG 34 in the "Kugelblende 30" ball mount was installed in the superstructure front of the Ausf.D and E. A "KZF2" periscopic gun sight was mounted in the ball mount. In the Ausf. B and C, a vision port and a pistol port replaced the machine gun and its ball mount in the super-structure front plate.

Eighty 7.5 cm KwK rounds and (after conversion to belt feed):

18 belt sacks with 150 = 2700 rounds (in Ausf. B and C),

21 belt sacks with 150 = 3150 rounds (in Ausf. D and E) of machine gun ammunition were carried.

Starting with the Ausf. D, the armored hull was widened 10 mm to 1860 mm, which increased the vehicles's overall width by 10 mm to 2840 mm. In the Ausf. D and E superstructure front plate, there was an MG 34 machine gun in a "Kugelblende 30" ball mount. For the driver's observation a driver's visor, "KFF" twin periscopic optics, and a vision port were installed. For the radio operator, in Ausf. B and C, two vision ports and a pistol port, in Ausf. D and E, the "KZF2" periscopic gun sight in the MG ball mount and a vision port.

In Ausf. B, C and D on the right side of the superstructure was a louvered entrance for combustion air for the motor. A sheet metal guard was installed inside the louvers for the engine air intake to catch bullet splash and shell fragments.

The superstructure front plate in the Ausf. B and C was made from a single straight plate with the driver's visor, radio operator's visor and pistol port all mounted in the same flat plane.

In the Ausf. D and E, the superstructure front plate in front of the radio operator was stepped to the rear. The driver could look and shoot to the right through a pistol port mounted in the short slanted sidewall.

Later, the superstructure front plates of the Ausf. D and E were strengthened by additional armor plates. On the Ausf. E, the additional plate ahead of the driver was welded with strips to the superstructure roof and bolted to the glacis plate. The additional 30 mm thick armor plate in front of the radio operator was bolted to a frame that was welded to the basic armor. The 20 mm thick additional armor plates on the superstructure and hull sides were bolted to the base side plates.

A rain gutter was attached over the driver's visor on the Ausf. C and D.

Beginning with Type D, two towing hooks and two chains were installed for attaching a towline to the hull rear.

In the Ausf. B and C cooling air intake and exhaust vents, three parallel horizontal louvers and two vertical supports were designed to retard projectiles and bullet splash from entering the engine compartment. This design was changed in the Ausf.D and E to two parallel horizontal louvers and four vertical guards with additional internal bullet splash guards.

The driver's two piece visor in the Ausf. B through D consisted of two overlapping sliding armored shutters. Their movement was reciprocal. In the Ausf. E, the driver's visor consisted of a single housing bolted to the driver's front plate and protected by a pivoting visor.

Panzerkampfwagen IV (7.5 cm), Ausf. D (Sd.Kfz.161)

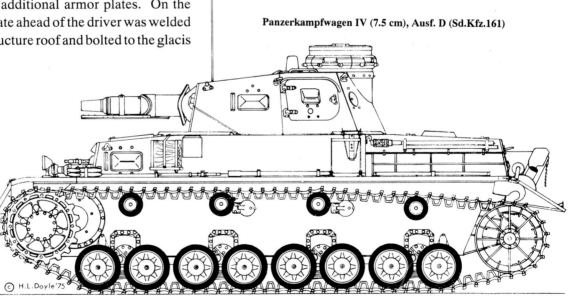

The driver's "KFF" twin periscopes provided the driver with an indirect view when the driver's visor was closed. Two holes were bored through the front wall of the driver's front plate above the driver's visor, providing apertures for the heads of the twin periscopes.

A "Kugelblende 30" ball mount was installed in the front superstructure of the Ausf. D and E. It allowed the radio operator to fire the MG 34. The ball mount consisted of a ball mount and its armored mantle. The ball, mounted so as to be traversable in all directions, had attachments on its rear to mount one MG 34 and the "KZF2" periscopic gun sight. In the Ausf. D, this included an attachment for saddle-magazine feed, which was later modified to hold cartridge belts in bags. In the Ausf. E, the mounting was originally designed for bagged cartridge-belt feed.

In the superstructure front of the Ausf. B and C, a pistol port was installed to the right of the vision port for the radio operator. A cover could be rotated to open the pistol port, allowing a machine pistol to be fired. A vision port with a vision slit in the armored cover was installed in the superstructure front of the Ausf. B and C, and afforded the radio operator a view to the front.

A pistol port without a vision slit was used in Ausf. D and E. It was located in the short slant superstructure front plate to the right front of the driver. It afforded the driver a view to the right. A vision port with a vision slit in the armored cover was mounted in the superstructure side walls to the left of the driver and to the right of the radio operator, to afford views to the sides.

In the side panniers and on the rear wall of the superstructure were racks for 26 7.5 cm rounds, with 54 more stored in racks mounted in the chassis, for a total of 80 rounds.

An outer armored mantle was bolted to the turret front plate of the Ausf. B and C, over the internal gun mantle, covering the gaps between the internal gun mantle and the front wall of the turret. A seal of leather and sheet metal was clamped in between the inner and outer mantles. Ausf. D and E had neither the internal gun mantle nor the seal. The gaps were covered by an external gun mantle with armor side shields.

In Ausf. D and E, a speaking tube was attached on the left side under the roof for communication between the commander and the gunner.

In the middle of the turret roof there was a ventilation opening, shielded and sealed by an armored cover. On both the right and left turret roof were round signal ports. The right signal port had a flat armored cover. A hood was mounted atop the left signal port.

The Ausf. E turret had a signal port only on the left side of the roof, while at the right front there was an opening cut for a fume extraction fan covered by an armor disc. In this version the ventilator opening with cover and the hood of the left signal opening were no longer installed.

When opened, the one-piece hatch covers in both turret sides were held in place by a bolt on each forward sidewall. The hatch covers of Type E were held open by a catch.

At each side there was a pistol port in the turret rear wall.

Four hooks were provided on the turret for use in installing and removing the turret. They could also be used for attaching camouflage materials. Later, a stowage box was fastened to the rear hooks to carry the crew's packs.

While the gun mantle for the Ausf. B and C was made of a half-cylindrical curved sheet of armor plate, closed at each end by sidewalls that carried the shield trunnions, the gun mantle used on the Ausf. D and E consisted of the shield, upper and lower mount sections, the two sidewalls and the rear wall. The sidewalls still bore the trunnions, which were mounted in bearings with bronze housings.

In the Ausf. D and E, the turret machine-gun attachment was moved farther to the front of the mount. The machine-gun barrel projecting through the gun mantle was protected by an armored cylinder welded to the gun mantle.

The commander's cupola, bolted to the turret rear of Ausf. B, C and D, consisted of a cylindrical mantle, five upper and five lower sliding shutters, an internal azimuth indicator ring and a two-piece hatch cover. The cupola afforded the commander an entry hatch as well as observation. The cylindrical mantle had five vision openings that could be partially or completely closed by the reciprocal action of the pairs of upper and lower sliding armor shutters.

In Ausf. E, the commander's cupola consisted of a cylindrical mantle, the five upper and five lower sliding armor shutters, the five side armor guards, the internal azimuth indicator ring and the two-piece hatch cover. The cylindrical mantle had five vision openings, each of which could be partially or completely closed by a pair of adjustable sliding armored shutters. The vision openings were flattened on the outside to allow the shutters to slide. The side guards were fastened to the outside between the vision slits. The upper and lower sliding shutters slid in the grooves in the sides of the side guards. As of Ausf. E, the turret sidewalls were lengthened and the new commander's cupola no longer cut into the rear wall of the turret.

The gasoline-electric auxiliary generator set in the Ausf. B, C and D included a DKW Type "PZW 600" engine which was equipped with a Framo VG-V carburetor. To

The oil-cooler and generator side of the HL 120 TRM engine designed and produced by Maybach.

Longitudinal and transverse drawings of the HL 120 engine.

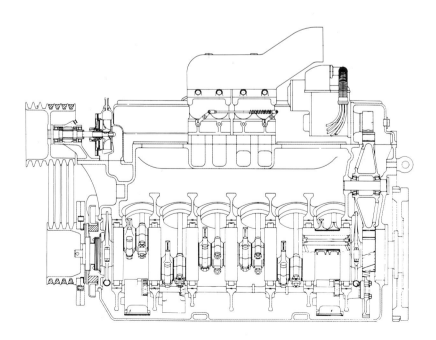

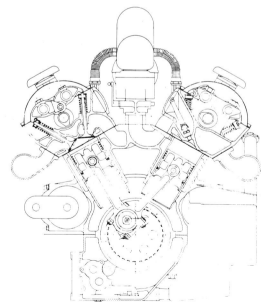

start the DKW engine there was a Bosch starter powered by the main engine generator. Starting with the Ausf. E, the DKW two-cylinder "ZW 500" engine, equipped with a SOLEX "26 BFV" carburetor, was used.

The manufacture of the 42 Ausf. B (Type 2/BW) began and the series was completed in 1938. These vehicles were equipped with Maybach "HL 120 TR" engines and ZF "SSG 76" transmissions. The first Panzerkampfwagen Ausf. C (Type 3/BW) appeared in 1938. As of chassis number 80 341, this version was powered by the Maybach "HL 120 TRM" engine. The end of this series of 140 Ausf. C was reached in August of 1939, when the last ten of these vehicles were produced. Completion of the first Ausf. D series began at the Krupp-Grusonwerk in September of 1939. There were 200 of this "Type 4/BW" in the initial Ausf. D contract. A subsequent contract for 48 more Ausf. D (Type 5/BW) followed. According to Document No. 1633/39 gK of November 11, 1939, the following numbers of Panzerkampfwagen IV were ordered: First series 35 units, second and third series 182 units, fourth series underway with 200 units, plus a fifth series of 48 units and a sixth series of 223 units were to be produced following the fourth and fifth series. Another 500 units were already ordered for the seventh series, but their completion date could not be predicted at that time.

Some of the Ausf. C chassis delivered for conversion to bridgelayers were subsequently completed as "Infanterie-Sturmsteg" assault bridges. In 1939, six chassis were set

The SSG 76 transmission designed and produced by the Zahnradfabrik Friedrichshafen.

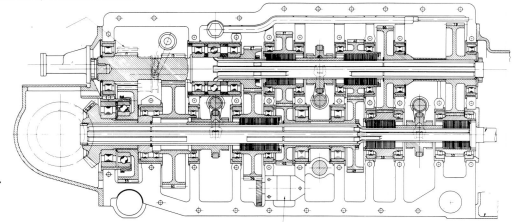

Longitudinal drawing of the transmission.

Typical of the time was the cap worn by the crews. As of January 1941, it was replaced by the normal black field cap.

The rear view of the Ausf. C shows the commander's cupola set into the rear turret wall, the smoke candle rack is mounted on the main engine exhaust muffler. The exhaust muffler for the auxiliary generator set is above it.

Panzerkampfwagen IV Ausf. D during maneuvers, with a Panzer III in the background. Ausf. D had a stepped superstructure front plate with projecting driver's compartment. The new gun mantle is easy to see.

aside for fitting bridgelaying superstructures. Another sixteen chassis followed for the same use in early 1940. These chassis were delivered to Magirus and Krupp for mounting modified superstructures with the bridgelayer components. Two of these chassis were returned in August of 1940 and converted back to tanks with turrets.

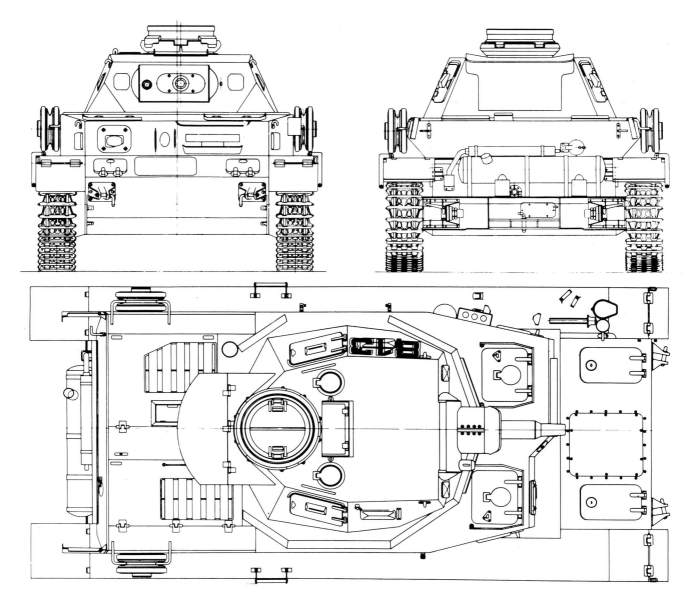

Three-view drawings of Panzerkampfwagen IV, Ausf. D.

One of the Ausf. D was armed experimentally with the 5 cm KwK 39 L/60 gun in 1941. The majority of the 248 Ausf. D were completed as tanks armed with the 7.5 cm KwK L/24. The sixth series, Ausf. E, began production in September 1940, and the last vehicles of this type were completed by May of 1941. Chassis based on the Panzer IV design were used by February of 1941 for the 10.5 cm Panzer-Selbstfahrlafette IVa [armored self-propelled gun carriage]. In conjunction with the conclusion of the Ausf. E series production in May 1941, some of the remaining Ausf. D bridgelayer chassis were rebuilt as tanks.

Starting with the Ausf. D, the Panzer IV had been fitted with new tracks. The tracks of Ausf. D and E could not be used on Ausf. A through C because of their higher center guides, but the older tracks could be used on the newer vehicles without difficulty.

Details of the front of an Ausf. D.

Panzerkampfwagen IV Ausf. D and E were regularly equipped with extra armor plate bolted onto the front and both sides of the superstructure. These photographs show such a vehicle at the Krupp-Grusonwerk in Magdeburg.

The Panzerkampfwagen IV Ausf. E had new idler wheels and a new design for the commander's cupola. Note also the additional armor plates bolted to the superstructure sides.

Panzerkampfwagen IV (7.5 cm) Ausf. E (Sd.Kfz.161)

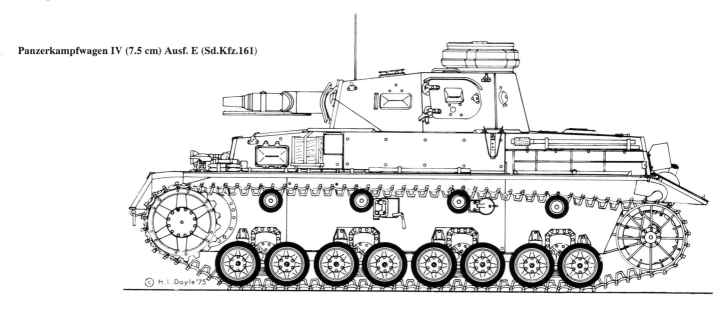

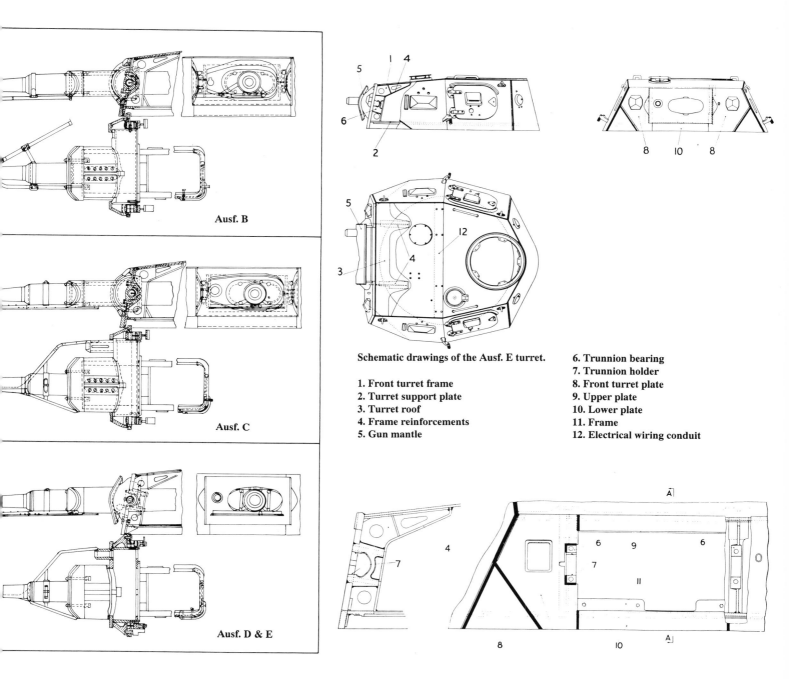

Ausf. B

Ausf. C

Ausf. D & E

Schematic drawings of the Ausf. E turret.

1. Front turret frame
2. Turret support plate
3. Turret roof
4. Frame reinforcements
5. Gun mantle
6. Trunnion bearing
7. Trunnion holder
8. Front turret plate
9. Upper plate
10. Lower plate
11. Frame
12. Electrical wiring conduit

After the Panzer Regiments were supplied with the Panzerkampfwagen IV starting in 1938 at a modest production rate. On September 1, 1939 there were 211 Panzerkampfwagen IV tanks available in the army inventory. After testing these vehicles in the Polish campaign, a statement appeared in the Heeresverordnungsblatt [Army Instruction Sheet] 1939 No. 685, stating that the "Panzerkampfwagen IV (7.5 cm) (Sd.Kfz.161)" had been declared ready for introduction and utilization on the basis of successful troop testing.

Nineteen Panzer IV tanks were lost to enemy action in the Polish campaign. In view of the meager capacity of the tank-production industry and the stockpiling of new tanks by the OKH, the rearmament of the Panzer Regiments with Panzerkampfwagen III and IV tanks proceeded slowly. At the beginning of the French campaign in May of 1940, the attacking Panzer Divisions had approximately 278 Panzer IV tanks available. The entire production for the year of 1940 amounted to only 278 Panzerkampfwagen IV. A message dated November 1, 1940 stated that the monthly production quota for the Panzer IV had been set at 30 units.

The new commander's cupola no longer cut into the rear turret wall, as the sidewalls had been lengthened. Instead of the earlier ventilator opening in the turret roof, a fume extraction fan was now installed.

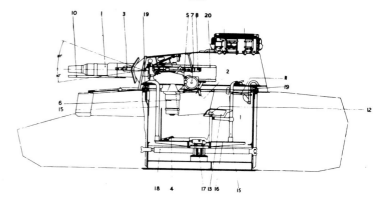

Fighting compartment of Panzerkampfwagen IV Ausf. E

1. 7.5 cm KwK L/24
2. Trigger mechanism
3. Turret machine gun
4. Machine gun trigger
5. Traversing handwheel
6. Traversing motor
7. Elevating handwheel
8. Telescopic gun sight "TZF"
9. Open gun sight
10. Antenna deflector
11. Commander's seat
12. Commander's footrest
13. Gunner's seat
14. Loader's seat
15. Turntable mount
16. Turntable base
17. Turntable bearing
18. Driveshaft
19. Turret turning bearing
20. Recoil deflector
21. Front observation ports
23. Turret azimuth (12-hour) indicator
24. Turret traverse lock

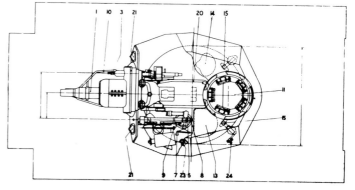

These photographs show details of the Panzerkampfwagen IV Ausf. C, which at this time (1939) was already being painted a solid dark gray. The national recognition symbol, the "Balkankreuz", had already been changed from that used in Poland.

This Pz.Kpfw.IV Ausf. D, serving in France in 1940 has been hit in the front hull plate by an armor piercing projectile.

From June 1 to September 1, 1940 the total number tanks in the army inventory rose from 4150 to 4833. In order to hasten the urgent outfitting of Panzer Divisions, Hitler ordered on August 20, 1940 that the Panzerkampfwagen III and IV and the "Panzerbefehlswagen" [armored command vehicle] be raised to a "special level" of manufacturing priority, whereas all armored vehicles of the "Schnellen Truppen" had previously been classified only at "Priority Level 1A."

For "Operation Sealion", the planned invasion of Britain, the Commander of the Army originally requested 180 underwater tanks. On August 1, 1940 there were 90 Panzer III tanks with 3.7 cm KwK guns, ten Panzer III with 5 cm KwK and 28 Panzer IV ready for service. In addition, twelve Sturmgeschütz were available.

In Poland, France, the Balkans, North Africa and Russia, the Panzer IV provided good support for the German troops.

For Operation "Sealion", Panzer IV tanks were outfitted to travel underwater. This photograph shows such a vehicle in Russia in 1941. On its turret it still has attachment points for the rubber cover intended to make the turret watertight.

The previously attained diving depth was seven meters; the required depth was 15 meters. An underwater speed of 5 to 7 km/hr was reached after the first tests. To some extent, the influence of buoyancy was a problem. By July 7, 1940 Wa Prüf 6 had conducted all of the related tests in Hamburg; only the watertightness tests were carried out at Aachen. On August 2, 1940 it was determined that the demonstrations of the underwater vehicles were satisfactory. The Schwimmpanzer II, also being prepared for service, made a very good impression. On the other hand, the special "Landwasserschlepper" [land-water tractor] had to be rejected as unusable.

On August 19, 1940 there were 152 Panzer III and 48 Panzer IV in all ready for the four special Panzer units. More than 52 Schwimmpanzer were not to be procured. What with technical breakdowns and other adjustments, the final numbers as of August 22, 1940 were 42 Panzer IV and 168 Panzer III, including eight units equipped with the 5 cm KwK gun. After "Operation Sealion" was given up, the vehicles divided among Eutin, Putlos, Bremen and Hamburg were almost all assigned to the 18th Panzer Division.

In order to restore the diving capability to some of these vehicles, four weeks were needed to remount the equip-ment, if they were required to achieve diving depths of 12 to 15 meters. F⸱⸱⸱⸱er depths of only six meters, sufficient for fording riv⸱⸱⸱ only a few days were necessary. These tests were introduced, and the preparations were entrusted to field workshops. As reported in contemporary accounts, parts of the 18th Panzer Division crossed the Bug River underwater on the morning of June 22, 1941, when the Russian campaign began.

The experiences gained in the previous campaigns had an effect on the 7th series (Ausf. F) of the Panzerkampfwagen IV, production of which started in May of 1941. In addition to Krupp, beginning with the Ausf. F, the firms of Vomag

Many improvements were introduced with the Ausf. F; the running gear was given new drive and idler wheels, and the basic frontal armor was 50 mm and the side armor 30 mm. These photographs show the vehicle from both sides.

The upper right photograph shows the straight front plate of the superstructure, which was reintroduced with the Ausf. F. A Fahrersehklappe 50 [driver's visor] and a Kugelblende 50 [ball mount] were installed. The additional track links which gave added protection are shown here in detail.

The new drive wheels of Ausf. F.

Panzerkampfwagen IV (7.5 cm)
Ausf. F1 (Sd.Kfz.161)

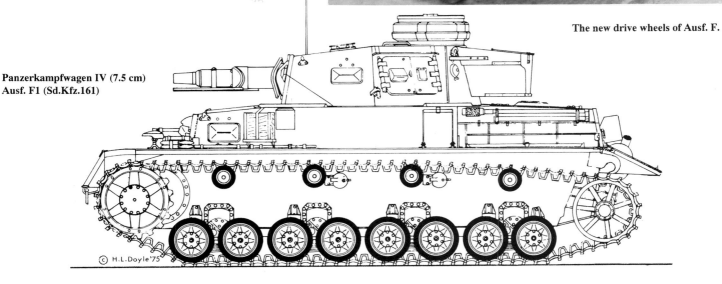

© H.L. Doyle '75

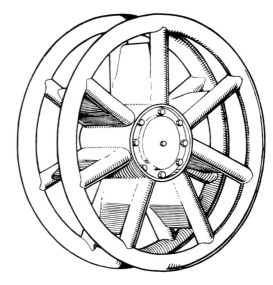

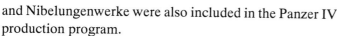

The idler wheel used through Ausf. E of Panzerkampfwagen IV. ◄◼

⬆ The idler wheels were welded. The photograph complements the drawing. ⬇

and Nibelungenwerke were also included in the Panzer IV production program.

Krupp built Panzerkampfwagen IV Ausf. F in Magdeburg from April 1941 through March 1942 with chassis numbers 82001-82395. Vomag completed 64 Panzerkampfwagen IV Ausf. F with chassis numbers 82501-82564 and the Nibelungenwerke built 13 Ausf. F with chassis numbers 82601-82613.

In June of 1941 there were problems with the start of the Ausf. F production. In this "Type 7/BW", the basic thickness for the frontal armor plates was established at 50 mm. The track width (track type Kgs 61/400/120) had been expanded from 380 to 400 mm. Changes had also been made to the drive and idler wheels of the running gear. The drive wheels, still made of cast steel, resembled the previous versions, but the hub was now recessed, and six spokes ran outward from the recessed hub to the toothed sprockets.

The idler wheels were changed much more. Instead of the previous cast steel version, now two wheels made of 60 mm steel tubes were welded together and linked by seven welded spokes.

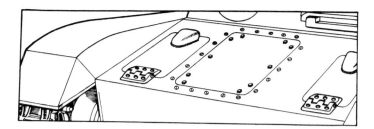

The previous one-piece entry hatch on the side of the turret (above) was replaced by a two-door version. The photographs below show the hatch closed and open.

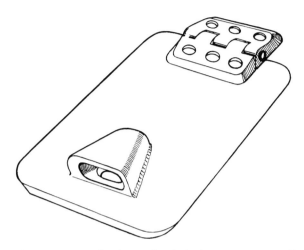

The maintenance access hatches on the glacis plate were given cowlings to protect the cooling air inlet for the steering brakes.

In addition, the two maintenance hatches on the glacis plate that provided access to the steering brakes were now each equipped with a ventilator cowl made of armor steel. The fighting weight had increased to 22.3 tons.

The front wall of the superstructure now ran straight across the tank. A "Fahrersehklappe 50" driver's visor was mounted on the left, the "Kugelblende 50" MG ball mount on the right, and a vision port in both sidewalls. The "Fahrersehklappe 50" consisted of a housing bolted to the front wall of the superstructure protected by a pivoting armor visor. The "KFF 2" driver's optics consisted of two double-angled periscopes with sight apertures in the superstructure front plate above the driver's visor.

The "Kugelblende 50" consisted of the ball mount itself, its cover and adapting ring. It served as the mount for an MG 34 with an armored mantle, belt feed, plus a "KZF2" periscopic gun sight.

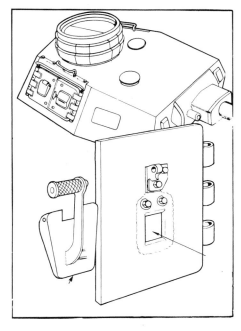

The pistol port in the rear half of the two-piece entry hatch can be seen in this drawing.

As before, there were 80 rounds on hand for the 7.5 cm KwK L/24 gun. For the two MG 34 machine guns there were 21 belt sacks, each with 150 rounds.

The armor for the turret was welded together out of several armor plates. The sidewalls were set at an angle of about 65 degrees, the front wall of the turret at 80 degrees, and the rear wall at about 75 degrees from the horizontal. The gun mantle was located in the front wall of the turret, with vision ports on both sides of the turret front. There was an entry hatch in each sidewall of the turret. These hatches were now closed by two-piece hatch covers. In each front half of these hatch covers there was a vision port with a vision slit and in each rear half there was a pistol port. To the left of the commander's cupola in the turret roof there was a circular opening for a signal port. At the right side of the turret roof was an electric fume extraction fan. The machine-gun mount in the gun mantle was modified; its mounting block was now fastened to the rear wall of the gun mantle.

The "TZF5b" telescopic gun sight was still used.

A listing of April 29, 1940 described the German-made armored vehicles in service as follows:

Panzerkampfwagen I (MG): [machine gun]
Panzerkampfwagen I (sIG): [heavy infantry gun]
Panzerkampfwagen I (Pz.Jäg. 4.7 cm): [tank destroyer]
Panzerkampfwagen I (Mun. Schlepper): [ammunition tractor]
Panzerkampfwagen II (KwK 2 cm: [20 mm tank gun]
Panzerkampfwagen II (F): [flame thrower]
Panzerkampfwagen II (Brückenleger): [bridgelayer]
Panzerkampfwagen III (Sfl. 7.5 cm): [self-propelled gun]
Panzerkampfwagen III (KwK 3.7 cm): [37 mm tank gun]
Panzerkampfwagen IV (KwK 7.5 cm): [75 mm tank gun]
Panzerkampfwagen IV (Brückenleger): [bridgelayer]
Panzerkampfwagen IV (Inf. Sturmsteg): [infantry assault bridge]

It was intended that 2160 Panzerkampfwagen IV tanks should be produced for the 36 Panzer divisions that were proposed on July 18, 1941. In fact, only 481 of these

For the first time, a not only equal but technically superior opponent was faced in the Russian campaign. Early success was gained only through superior tactics. This photograph shows Panzerkampfwagen III and IV tanks carrying infantrymen before an attack.

This photograph from the Nibelungenwerke shows the last Porsche Tiger chassis on the BW assembly line. Just behind it, full scale production of Panzer IV is underway.

BW tanks on the assembly line in St. Valentin, Lower Austria. The ammunition racks can be seen on the tank in front.

This series of photographs shows tracks being mounted at a factory. Details of the running gear can also be seen.

Before turrets were installed, the vehicles were broken in on the factory grounds. A weight was carried equivalent to the weight of the turret. The "Kugelblende 50" ball mount has not yet been installed.

vehicles were built in 1941. The Krupp-Gruson AG in Magdeburg-Buckau, reported completion of a total of 400 Panzer IV tanks in the period from October 1940 to September 1941.

On July 1, 1941 the total number of Panzer IV on hand was 531 units. What with losses in action, this number had risen to only 552 units by April 1, 1942.

The expansion of tank production capacity, introduced in 1940 was pushed emphatically, according to a communique (Staff 1a No. 1565/40 gKdos of August 17, 1940). In St. Valentin, Lower Austria, the Nibelungenwerk was built by the Steyr-Daimler-Puch AG. The planning of this factory under the direction of the Steyr-Daimler-Push AG was carried out through the cooperation of the Heeres Waffenamt and the machine and construction department of the Steyr firm. The total building costs were estimated at 65 million Reichsmarks. The production layout was based on the ALKETT firm's experience. Up to 150 tanks per month were to be produced. In September of 1940, all Steyr departments were transferred to St. Valentin, where the first work undertaken was the repair of Panzer III tanks. On account of the severe winter of 1939-1940, the beginning of construction at the Nibelungenwerke had been postponed until March 1940. In February of 1941 the first part, Hall VI, was finished, in March 1941 Hall V, which made the commencement of tank spare-part production possible. By the end of March 1941, 12.4 tons of spare parts for Panzer II and 28.6 tons for Panzer III had been produced. Only in the late fall of 1941 were Halls I and II and the office building finished. The number of employees totaled 4800. Compared to the third quarter of 1941, the spare-parts production in the fourth quarter had risen from 16.6 to 17.2 tons for Panzer III and from 197.6 to 358.9 tons for Panzer IV. This meant that the start of series production was largely prepared for. As of 1941, the production of road wheels and planetary gears had also begun, with the products sent to Krupp-Gruson in Magdeburg for the Panzer IV tanks assembled there. In the last quarter of 1941, Nibelungenwerk began Panzer IV production in St. Valentin, completing three new Panzerkampfwagen IV Ausf. F and repairing one older Panzerkampfwagen IV.

The Vogtländische Maschinenfabrik AG in Plauen (Vomag) set up a new production facility of 43,000 square meters in 1940-41. Both factories were to concentrate on Panzer IV production.

In addition, the MIAG firm in Braunschweig expanded its tank-producing facilities at this time, while the Klöckner-Humboldt-Deutz AG had already begun to produce spare parts for tanks in April of 1940.

On April 3, 1941, details of how to carry more ammunition and fuel in tanks were taken up. Attempts were made to increase the range of tanks, particularly in reference to "Operation Barbarossa", which was about to commence. In terms of fuel, a solution was found in the form of fuel tanks mounted on single-axle trailers. No solution to the problem of carrying more ammunition was introduced at that time. On May 14, 1941 it was reported that by June 10 about 1860 fuel-tank trailers for tanks, equipped with pumps would be available, increasing the tanks' radius of action by 100%. According to a report dated May 22, 1941, 1800 fuel-tank trailers for Panzer III tanks were ready by June 9, but the completion of trailers for Panzer IV could not be expected before the end of June.

To prepare for the Russian campaign, German tanks were equipped with single-axle trailers that could carry two barrels of fuel to increase their radius of action. This photograph shows a Panzer IV in the first weeks of the campaign, with equipment atop the rear deck and identification flag spread over it.

The Panzer troops were supplied by fuel tank trucks (Sd.Kfz.5) that could carry some 3600 liters of fuel. They were generally built on the Krupp L 3 H 163 chassis.

At the same time, the question of increasing the wading capability of the Panzer III and IV was raised. Attempts were to be made to attain a fording capability of four meters.

Among others, fuel tank trucks (Sd.Kfz.5) were available to the Panzer units for the purpose of fuel supply; they were built on the chassis of the medium open bed truck, which had off-road capability. The tank capacity was some 3600 liters. The Krupp Type "L 3 H 163" truck was most often used for this purpose.

In a discussion with Hitler at the Berghof (WaA No. 524/41 gKdos Wa J Rü (WuG Chef 31.5.41), the question of rearming the Panzer IV was taken up. It was considered necessary to increase the penetrating power of guns in the existing tank program in every way possible

New vehicles were steadily shipped to the troops. The Panzer IV, like all military equipment, had a base coat of "Dunkelgelb" paint during the latter half of the war. Any additional camouflage was applied by the troops themselves.

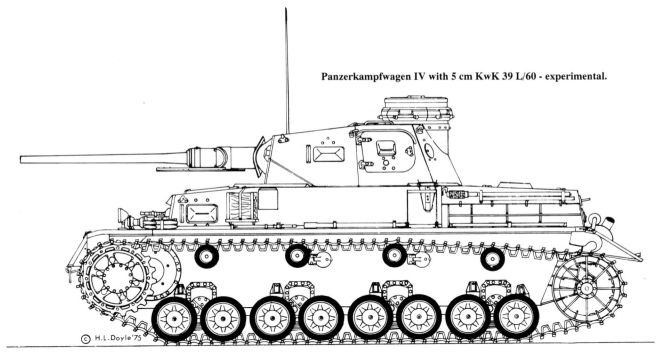

Panzerkampfwagen IV with 5 cm KwK 39 L/60 - experimental.

A Panzer IV with the 5 cm KwK 39 L/60 installed as an experiment. This photograph shows the vehicle during winter testing at St. Johann in Tirol, January 13, 1942.

The Krupp firm had a contract to introduce a Panzerkampfwagen IV with a 5 cm Pak 38 (instead of the 7.5 cm KwK L/24) by November 15, 1941. The Waffenamt was asked to contact the Krupp firm and achieve earlier completion of this work. The first new version of the 5 cm KwK L/42 gun was fired on August 1, 1941. The planned use of a "bottle cartridge" in the 5 cm KwK was not supposed to be limited to this one gun, if it brought good results and the feared difficulties with the cartridge were overcome, but to be expanded to include the Pak 38 as well.

Dr. Hacker stated that, with a decision on the Krupp solution by August 1941, the Nibelungenwerk could deliver some 80 Panzerkampfwagen IV with Pak 38 guns by the spring of 1942. The Nibelungenwerk were already preparing for their installation.

This solution was already superseded by the events in Russia. On November 18, 1941 a contract (No. 917/41 gKdos Wa Prüf 4) was awarded by the Waffenamt to the Krupp firm for the production of a successor weapon to the short 7.5 cm tank gun previously used in the Panzer IV; this contract was to be urgently filled in co-operation with Rheinmetall-Borsig AG. It called for the development of a KwK 44 (later called KwK 40) with a barrel length of 3218 mm (L/43). The initial velocity for the "Panzergranate 40" [tungsten carbide, subcaliber armor piercing projectile] was to be 990 meters per second. The maximum range was increased from 6500 to 8100 meters.

Mass production of these weapons was expected by March 1942.

An original document to the Commander of the Army, signed by Generalfeldmarschall Keitel on November 14, 1941, already acknowledged the influence of the reports coming from the Eastern Front: ". . . the Führer considers it necessary in view of our most sharply intensified and limited production potential to limit the "tank program" in terms of the various kinds and decide on the future types. In the process, development now underway that must be eliminated anyway during this war should also result in the unburdening of the design bureau of the firms and free engineers, making them available for production. The Führer requires such a simplification and limitation or normalization of motors, gearboxes, road wheels, tracks and other components.

The Führer has the following four basic types more or less in mind:
   –a fast (reconnaissance) armored vehicle,
   –a medium tank (based on the present Panzer IV),
   –a heavy tank (Porsche and Henschel), and
   –a heaviest tank.

The Führer wishes to make this decision personally and wants Oberst Fichtner to talk it over with Professor Porsche at the FHQ after the coming trip to the front . . ."

The Panzer I, II, III and IV tanks that saw service in Africa between 1941 and 1943 had already been fitted with modified engine cooling systems before being shipped out. Felt filters were attached outside the engine compartment or as pre-filters inside the chassis. The vehicles thus modified were given the added designation (Tp): tropic.

On March 16, 1942 Hitler expressed his agreement to the snowplow program. The experiences of the first Russian winter had proved the efficacy of such equipment. Ongoing tests were carried out at the winter school of the Panzer troops in St. Johann. On April 4, 1942 Speer reported on the development of a small snowplow attached to the front of a normal tank; it moved the snow under the tracks. This development was continued at Hitler's urging. In October of 1942 the first snow-plowing equipment was ready for operational use.

On April 4, 1942 Hitler asked that a Panzer IV with the long 7.5 cm gun be presented at his headquarters as soon as possible, and on April 15 Hitler showed himself to be satisfied with the developmental stages of the Panzer IV with the 7.5 cm KwK 40 gun that he had been shown.

The first long barrels were installed in the Panzerkampfwagen IV. For better differentiation, the vehicles with the short guns were designated "Ausf. F1", while the new Panzer IV with the longer guns bore the designation "Ausf. F2."

A Panzer IV before being shipped to North Africa. Additional water containers have been stowed on the turret roof.

To remove obstacles and clear roads in winter, tanks were also equipped with plow blades. This photograph shows a Panzer IV with an off-road plow. 1. Plow, 2. Panzer IV.

Hitler attends the presentation of the first Panzer IV equipped with the long 7.5 cm gun. The barrel had a ball muzzle brake.

The tanks armed with this gun were designated "Ausf. F2", since the tank was identical to its predecessor except for its armament.

Panzerkampfwagen IV (7.5 cm KwK L/43) Ausf. F2 (Sd.Kfz.161/1).

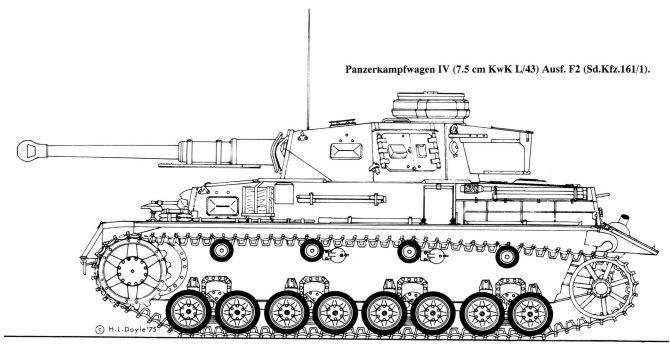

© H.L. Doyle '75

The first Ausf.F2 was completed in March of 1942, with the assembly of only one Panzerkampfwagen IV. Further Panzerkampfwagen IV with the long 7.5 cm KwK 40 L/43 were completed by Krupp with chassis numbers 82396-82500, by Vomag with chassis numbers 82565-82600, and by the Nibelungenwerke with chassis numbers 82614-82700. Production converted to the Ausf.G in the Summer of 1942.

The 7.5 cm KwK 40 L/43 originally had a single acting, ball-shaped muzzle brake. Thirty-two rounds were stored in the superstructure and 55 in the hull, for a total of 87 7.5 cm KwK 40 rounds stored in the Ausf.F2. In the superstructure, there were 13 sacks of machine-gun ammunition hanging on the right wall, with four more ahead of the radio operator's seat and four to the right on the turntable. For use with the 7.5 cm KwK 40 L/43 there was a "TZF5f" telescopic gun sight.

The fighting weight of the Ausf. F2 had increased to 23.6 tons. The price of the vehicle (without weapons) was 103,462 Reichsmarks.

One of the F2 vehicles in action. This weapon allowed the Panzer IV to fight against all enemy tanks in use at that time.

In the period from October 1941 to September 1942, the Krupp-Gruson AG produced a total of 533 Panzer IV. According to a memo of January 24, 1942, the Panzerkampfwagen IV had been built in 1941 at a monthly rate of 40 units. In 1942 their production quota of 57 units per month was exceeded by actually producing 65 Panzer IV tanks in December 1942. From this point on, the Panzer IV entered large scale production. In November 1941, Nibelungenwerk in St. Valentin began Panzerkampfwagen IV production. This factory set out to produce 16% of the total production of this, then considered to be the most important German tank. Vomag had taken up production of the Panzer IV and completed 40 of the vehicles by the end of 1941.

Generaloberst Heinz Guderian reported that twelve Panzer IV tanks with 80 mm front armor plate had been requested for the landing in Malta that was planned for March of 1942.

On May 24, 1942 Hitler ordered that all Panzer IV tanks with the 7.5 cm KwK 40 were to be fitted with additional armor plate, provided that this did not cause any essential delay in production. If subsequent experience with this additional armor should astonishingly show bad characteristics, then the vehicles produced to that point would still be usable. On June 29, 1942, Hitler decided that the added armor for the Panzer IV was to be used only to a limited extent. A monthly production of 16 units was planned.

The National Socialist Vehicle Corps (NSKK) provided some training for tank drivers during the war. The photograph shows one of the corps' training tanks, which were normally used without a turret.

After the long gun was introduced, backfitting the latest modifications to rebuilt Panzer IV made exact identification of the different versions difficult. The vehicle shown here, in NSKK service, has the offset front panel with additional armor, the KwK 40 gun, and Schürzen skirts on the turret.

Production of the Panzerkampfwagen IV (7.5 cm) (Sd.Kfz.161/1) Ausf. G began in mid 1942. By the Summer of 1943, Krupp-Grusonwerk, Vomag, and Nibelungenwerk had produced 1700 Panzerkampfwagen IV with the 7.5 cm KwK 40 in the chassis number series from 82701 through 84400.

The front of the superstructure and hull of a portion of Ausf. G production series were strengthened by additional 30 mm thick armor plates. A double chambered muzzle brake was also introduced for the 7.5 cm KwK 40 L/43. The warning lights, which indicated in the previous versions of the Panzer IV when the tank gun extended beyond the profile of the vehicle, were eliminated beginning with the Ausf. G.

In June of 1942 an order was issued that called for strengthening the front armor of the Panzer IV to 80 mm. As of August 15, the final version of the 7.5 cm KwK 40, with a barrel length of L/48, was available for testing. From then on, all Panzer IV vehicles that were repaired in Germany were to be rearmed with the 7.5 cm KwK 40.

In this respect it must still be noted that all vehicles that were sent back to Germany to be repaired during the war were always brought up to the latest technical level. It was quite possible to install improved assemblies, additional armor and more powerful weapons in these older vehicles. A precise technical identification was thus made considerably more difficult.

Panzerkampfwagen IV (7.5 cm KwK L/43) Ausf. G (Sd.Kfz.161/1)

© H.L.Doyle '75

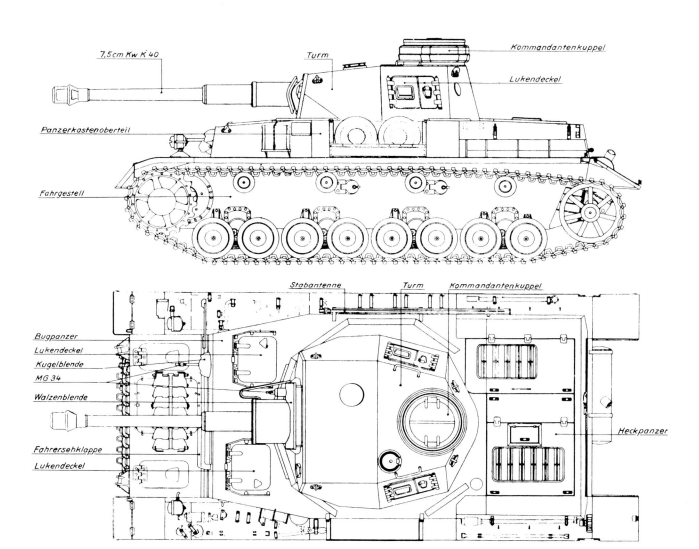

7,5 cm Kw K 40

Turm

Kommandantenkuppel

Lukendeckel

Panzerkastenoberteil

Fahrgestell

Stabantenne

Turm

Kommandantenkuppel

Bugpanzer

Lukendeckel

Kugelblende

MG 34

Walzenblende

Fahrersehklappe

Lukendeckel

Heckpanzer

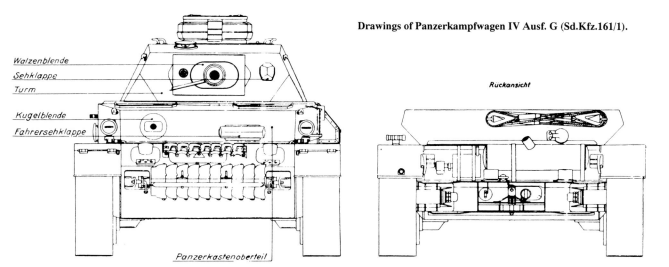

Walzenblende

Sehklappe

Turm

Kugelblende

Fahrersehklappe

Panzerkastenoberteil

Rückansicht

Drawings of Panzerkampfwagen IV Ausf. G (Sd.Kfz.161/1).

Panzerkampfwagen IV Ausf. G used the 7.5 cm KwK 40 with double chambered muzzle brake. The photographs show three sides of the vehicle.

Left page, right column: Photographs show the interior of the turret with the gunner's seat. The handwheels for traverse and elevation and telescopic gun sight are easy to see.
◀

The loader's view of the breech of the gun, secured with the travel lock.
◀

Upper right: The radio operator's seat in the Panzer IV, with weapons removed. At left is the transmission, in front the housing of the steering brakes. ▶

The front of Ausf. G shows the weapon installation, the driver's and radio operator's hatches, the side vision port and the steering-brake ventilator opening.

After the troops had received the vehicles, they made changes to the exterior of the Panzer IV. Here a pole is carried to make crossing ditches easier. Note also the antenna deflector under the turret machine gun.
◀

The Panzer IV proved their reliability in all theaters of war. Added pieces of equipment always changed the appearance of the vehicles.
◀

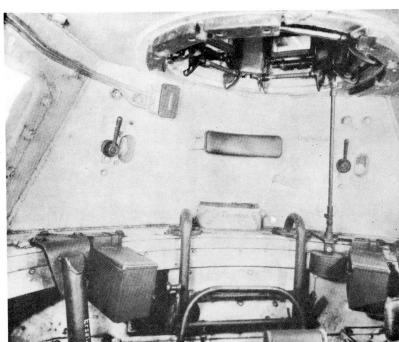

The back wall of the turret with the commander's seat and cupola.
▶

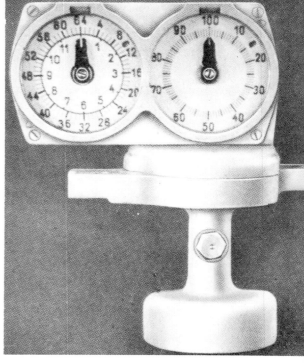

The turret azimuth indicator in the Panzer IV.

Upper left: The fighting compartment of Panzerkampfwagen IV.

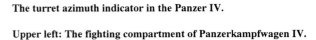

The layout of the Ausf. G fighting compartment.

A stowage rack for the long rounds.

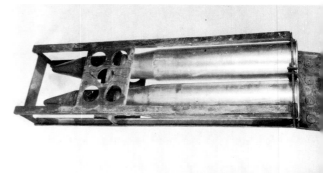

On October 14, 1942 it was reported to Hitler that a considerable number of Panzer IV tanks would be equipped with winter tracks before winter began. According to the plans at hand, some 75% would be equipped by January 1, 1943. Hitler considered it important that vehicles used by the Heeres Gruppen Nord and Mitte [Army Groups North and Center] in particular be fully equipped for winter.

At the same time, Hitler stressed his standpoint that what with the growing strength of enemy tanks, at least a part of the Panzer IV production must continue to have frontal armor up to 80 mm thick, this being of extraordinary value.

According to the troop reports at hand on November 8, 1942, the additional 30 mm thick armor plates on the Panzer IV had proved itself in many cases despite the resulting technical problems of driving them. Since the new British 6-Pounder (57 mm) antitank gun could still penetrate the front (50 mm) of the Panzer IV at a range of 1000 meters, it was decided that 50% of Panzer IV production be fitted with the 30 mm thick additional armor plates.

On December 3, 1942 short-term tests were ordered for the purpose of determining changes to the Panzer IV's running characteristics after conversion to sloped armor and reinforcement of the bow and bottom. These tests were to be concluded by December 16, 1942, since at that time it would be necessary to make a decision in order to guarantee conversion by the summer of 1943.

A document issued on December 15, 1942 described a spotlight for Panzer III and IV, which was supposed to be used in night combat.

Of the 994 Panzer IV tanks built in 1942, Krupp-Gruson built about 571. The Nibelungenwerk in St. Valentin produced 186 in 1942 and the year's production at Vomag numbered 237 Panzer IV tanks.

The production of hulls, upper body armor and turrets, which had formerly been done almost exclusively by the firms of Krupp in Essen and Eisen- und Hüttenwerke in Bochum, was transferred from 1942 on more and more to the Austrian area and the firms of Gebr. Böhler & Co., Kapfenberg, and Eisenwerke Oberdonau (today VOEST) in Linz. Until that point, Krupp in Essen had turned out a weekly quantity of about 25 hulls, upper bodies and turrets for the Panzer IV.

The frontal armor of the vehicles was strengthened to 80 mm by bolting on additional plates. The side vision ports were eliminated.

A comparison of the raw-material needs for Panzer III and IV (in kg, without weapons, optics and radios) gave the following results:

Panzerkampfwagen III	Raw Material	Panzerkampfwagen IV
39000	Iron (Fe)	39000
1.4	Tin (Sn)	1.2
60.1	Copper (Cu)	195.1
90.4	Aluminum (Al)	238
71.1	Lead (Pb)	63.3
49.1	Zinc (Zn)	66.4
–	Magnesium (Mg)	0.15
125	Potassium (K)	116.3

Of the required iron listed above, 20211 kg were unalloyed and 18752 kg alloyed sheet metal, with 15841 kg heavy and medium sheets and 852 kg thin sheets.

Krupp was the only producer of armor plate for the German Navy but also produced a large part of the armor plate for the Army. After 1939, no more armor steel was produced for the Navy except that used in ballistic tests. The two rolling mills available at the Krupp works produced 12,000 tons of steel plate per month, its width being 4 or 4.5 meters.

In addition, sufficient facilities were available for heat-treating, equipping and checking. Sheets from 10 to 350 mm thick could be rolled. Since 1939, armor plate from 16 to 50 mm thick had been produced. The greatest armor thickness for armored vehicles was 180 mm, though only small quantities of this thickness were produced.

The following table shows the composition of the armor steel used by Krupp toward the end of the war. This was not Krupp's own alloy, but the material composition required by the Waffenamt:

Thickness in mm	Resistance kg/mm²	Carbon C	Silicon Si	Manganese Mn	Chromium Cr	Nickel Ni
5-15	150-170	.23	1.20	.80	1.10	–
16-30	105-120	.45	.65	.60	.60	–
35-50	95-110	.45	.65	.80	.90	–
55-80	85-100	.45	.65	1.00	1.05	–
85-120	75-90	.42	.35	.75	1.75	–
125-160	75-90	.35	.35	.75	2.50	1.25
165-200	75-90	.35	.35	.75	3.00	1.00

In order to save nickel, Krupp used the following alloy instead of that shown above: C .35, Si .35, Mn .40, Cr 2.5, and molybdenum (Mo) .45. Heat-treating equipment for cast armor steel had been installed at the Krupp works shortly before the war began.

The last armor plate produced by Krupp showed the following composition:

Thickness in mm	Resistance kg/mm²	Carbon C	Manganese Mn	Silicon Si	Phosphorus P	Chromium Cr
10-40	80-95	.30	.65	.35	.030	1.35
50-120	75-90	.37	.75	.35	.030	2.30
over 120	65-80	.37	.50	.35	.030	2.40

Nickel (Ni)	Treatment	
–	Water	Phosphorus (P) and Sulfur (S)
–	Oil	compound was maximum
1.95	Oil	additive.

Before the war, Krupp used the following alloy for armor plate of strengths from 5 to 100 mm:

C .35, Mn .40, Si .35, Cr 2.50, Mo .45. It was treated with water.

The winter experience gained in Russia resulted in the installation of a so-called "cooling water exchanger." This apparatus made it possible to pump hot water from one vehicle to another to avoid problems in starting motors in cold weather.

On January 5, 1943, Hitler decided, despite negative test reports, that the Panzer IV should soon be built with an angled bow plate 100 mm thick. Until it was scheduled to enter production, all Panzer IV tanks were to be fitted with 80 mm front armor. The 47 Panzer IV tanks ready for delivery at Magdeburg should therefore be fitted with front

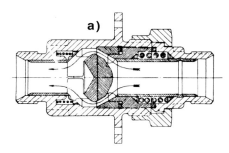

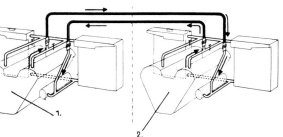

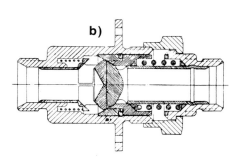

For conditions in Russia, a system of transmitting cooling water was developed that made it possible to add hot cooling water to cold vehicles. This photograph shows the vehicle to be warmed; the tank supplying the warm water always had to be situated lower.

1. Tank to be warmed
2 + 3. Water transfer hose
4. Tank supplying warm water

Left center: The water transfer system. 1. Motor to be warmed. 2. Warm motor.

The hose couplings for water transfer. a. Shutoff valve, opened. 2. Shutoff valve, closed.

a)

b)

Vehicles could also be supplied from outside with a Panzer Cooling-Water Heater 42. The schematic drawings show the layout.

1. Radiator
2. Cold-water return connection from motor
3. Hot-water supply connection to motor
4. Radiator
5. Oil cooler
6. Cylinder block

The photograph at left complements the schematic drawings.

1. Upper water line
2. Cold-water return connection from motor
3. Shutoff valve for one radiator
4. Warm-water supply connection to motor

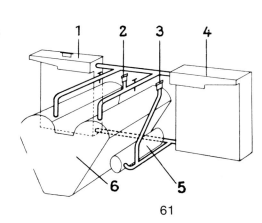

61

armor immediately, since they were intended for special use.

Hitler took up the question of enlarging the tanks' radius of action again on January 5, 1943, with the comment that sufficient fuel supply was one of the most decisive questions in tank use. Therefore the already insti-tuted developments must be brought to a conclusion, specifically by using tank trailers and additional fuel tanks that could be jettisoned.

On January 18, 1943 Hitler decided, on the basis of the decisive significance of the tank weapon, on the immediate introduction of all those measures that would lead to an

Details of the Schürzen skirts mounted on the turret are shown in these close-up photos.

A Panzerkampfwagen IV Ausf. H, fully equipped. The added Schürzen plates on the sides were removable, those on the turret were fixed in place.

increase, as soon as possible, in the production of tanks.

For this purpose he had granted Speer the appropriate powers. Hitler was informed that in transition, and in fact for about the first four months of 1943, an increase beyond the Adolf Hitler Program would presumably be possible only in the production of Panzer IV tanks and Sturmgeschütz. As soon as possible thereafter, the measures being introduced would also result in a considerable increase in the Panther tank program.

Speer brought it to Hitler's attention that any increase that was at all possible would, in transition, require a considerably greater concentration in component production at only a few construction facilities, in some cases at only one facility. Hitler stated that he agreed to such a transition, but requested that all the measures that would assure the long-term success of the program, even in the face of external influences, be introduced simultaneously.

During the required time for single facility production, Hitler's previous request had to be introduced at once, namely that for every component produced, a transitional supply to the extent of one month's production be prepared, and that machines needed to produce this component be located at a different place.

For the winter war in Russia, "heavy sled trailers for tracked vehicles" like those used by the Russians were introduced as of 1943 for the transport of escort infantry and supplies.

At the Nibelungenwerke, the monthly production of 50 Panzerkampfwagen IV in January 1943 was raised to 70 units by March. The conversion of the production tanks for the new commander's cupola caused a delay, since the delivery of cupolas from the Eisenwerke Oberdonau GmbH in Linz could not be kept on schedule because of delays in raw material deliveries. Production came to a standstill with the 44th tank. Thanks to delivery of commanders' cupolas by truck from the Vomag works in Plauen and the use of all available personnel, the prescribed delivery quota could be met.

On March 6, 1943, Hitler was informed of the favorable results of firing tests on Schürzen side skirts to date. In addition to the ongoing fitting of Schürzen skirts to all newly produced Panzer IV tanks, all tanks of this type already in service and under repair were to be fully equipped in the shortest possible time. A planned date for complete equipping was to be set quickly. On March 19, 1943 the first Panzer IV with Schürzen skirts on its sides and turret was exhibited.

On March 9, 1943 Generaloberst Heinz Guderian gave a report at the Führer's headquarters on the state and development of the German tank forces. In it he declared that the equipment of the armored forces at this point in time depended exclusively on the Panzer IV, for which reason the further production of these vehicles, including the years of 1944-45, had to be continued at full speed.

Thereupon, in April 1943, the industry received appropriate instructions. But attempts were made constantly to circumvent this order and to convert Panzer IV production to that of Sturmgeschütz, wherein the tendency of these efforts to adapt the offensive character of the tank weapon to the defensive warfare of 1943-45 became more and more obvious.

On April 3, 1943 Hitler declared the great tank production program (ending with 1955 tanks in the fourth quarter of 1943) to be absolutely necessary. It was to be taken for granted that the necessary quantities of iron could be made available if the full-capacity production of iron could take place as planned. On the basis of a conference held on April 11, 1943, the further construction of Panzer IV tanks at full capacity should be assured in 1944 as well, until "full-capacity production of the Panther tank could be established with absolute certainty."

In the meantime, in the Summer of 1943, production of the Panzerkampfwagen IV (7.5 cm) (Sd.Kfz.161/2) Ausf. H had begun at the three assembly facilities. These were produced by Krupp-Grusonwerk, Vomag, and Nibelungenwerk in the chassis number series from 84401 through about 89600. While most of the Ausf.H chassis were completed as tanks with superstructures and turrets, some of the chassis were diverted for assembly as Sturmpanzer and Sturmgeschütz.

The front armor now measured 80 mm, and the vehicle carried the 7.5 cm KwK 40 L/48 gun. The fighting weight

Panzerkampfwagen IV (7.5 cm KwK L/48) Ausf. H (Sd.Kfz.161/2)

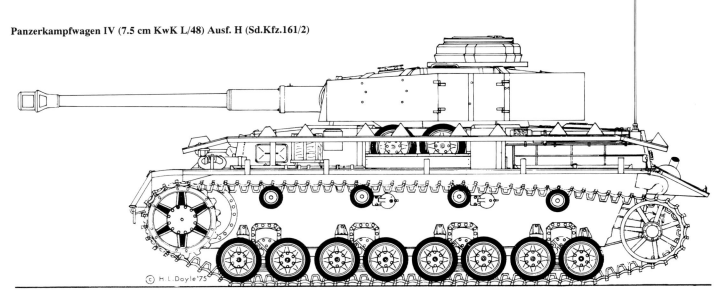

© H.L.Doyle '75

1589 b

Right: The application of "Zimmerit" anti-magnetic compound can be seen in these front and rear views. The antenna had been moved to the left rear.

Bottom, left page: This overhead view of the same vehicle shows the Schürzen mounts and the additional air-intake filter on the right side.

Lower left: The Schürzen skirts, hanging loosely, were easily lost in action.

Lower right: Schürzen plates were later replaced by wire mesh skirts.

was 25 tons. The chassis remained almost unchanged, with only modified drive and idler wheels being used during the course of production. Some of the return rollers, made until then with full rubber tires, were replaced by those with steel surfaces. In addition, the ZF SSG 76 six-speed manual transmission continued to be used. It had synchromesh provision for all gears except first and reverse. The forward gears were in constant mesh and were fitted with diagonally toothed gears for low noise.

The turret vision ports, like those in the turret access hatches, had been eliminated, having been made useless in any case by the installation of the additional 8 mm Schürzen skirts on the turret. In addition, these vehicles were produced with the 5 mm Schürzen side skirts already installed. The commander's cupola was closed by a one-piece round hatch cover.

As of March 1944, Panzer IV tanks were also converted to Panzerbefehlswagen [armored command vehicles]. They were armed exactly like the tanks but had additional radio equipment and antennas. The loader also acted as a second radio operator. From March 1944 to September of that year, 89 units were made out of repaired vehicles, while eight more were taken from new production. It was planned that the mounts for the additional radio equipment and antennas would be included in the new production, so that if necessary the vehicles could be converted for use as command vehicles by the troops.

For armored artillery units the Panzerbeobachtungswagen IV [armored observation vehicle] was created, likewise carrying the 7.5 cm KwK L/48 gun as its primary weapon. Unlike the tank, it had an extendable periscope, passing through the turret roof, installed for the commander's use. Also installed in the turret roof, near the turret ventilator, was a second antenna. The normal antenna, at the left side of the engine compartment in the rear, was eliminated, but in its place a star antenna had been installed at the right rear of the engine compartment. Of these vehicles, most of which were created from rebuilt, repaired Panzer IV. Ninety-six units were supplied to the troops from September 1944 to March 1945.

During Ausf. H production, the drive wheels were changed. This photograph shows details of them. The sprockets were replaceable.

The "Panzerbefehlswagen IV" had a periscope in the turret to the left of the commander, plus a second antenna near the fume extraction fan armor cover.

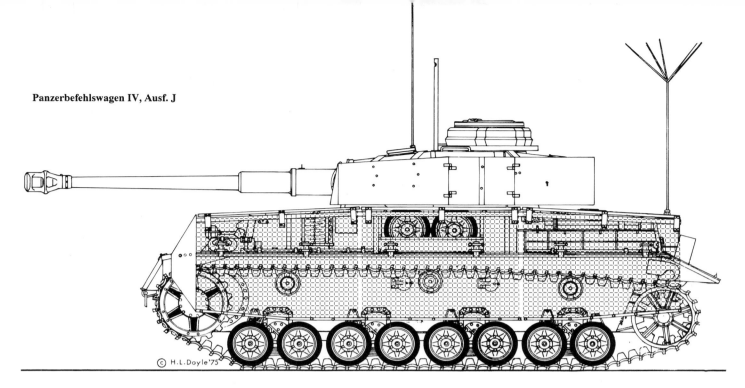

Panzerbefehlswagen IV, Ausf. J

On May 4, 1943 Hitler called for the statistics of actual tank production for the month of April in comparison to the production quotas that had been set for the period up to May 12. Since the combat activities planned for the coming summer were decisively dependent on a superior number of tanks, Hitler expected that everything would be done not only to equal these figures but to exceed them whenever possible. This was particularly true for the months of May, June and July 1943. At the same time, Hitler again called attention to the small number of tanks being repaired both at the front and in Germany. He expected a prompt suggestion that could be implemented by the Generalinspekteur der Panzer Truppen (Guderian). The greatest possible responsibility of the industry was to be involved so that both an increase in the number of tanks repaired and a quicker and therefore more dependable provision to meet spare-parts needs could be attained.

On August 5, 1943 it was decided that an appropriately reduced production program for the manufacture of tanks and related types such as recovery tanks, low-loader trailers and the like be instituted for the transitional period. To overcome the shortage of raw material for ongoing armor production at the time, it was suggested that the production quotas for a series of devices be cut back for a time, so as to make material available for the ongoing production of machine tools, buildings, facilities and equipment at that time.

Thus in the first months of 1943 the completion of the considerably expanded "Adolf Hitler Tank Program" was the most urgent task, the focal point of all weapons production. Despite the increased production of new tank types and of Panzerjäger [tank destroyers], the production of the Panzer IV remained the heart of all German tank manufacture. Of the 3054 Panzer IV tanks that had been produced in Germany in 1943, about 1378, or 44%, of them came from the Nibelungenwerke and constituted some 11% of the total German tank production. The assembly works in St. Valentin were supplied with 1305 hulls and upper bodies and 1275 turrets by the iron works in Linz. The Böhler firm in Kapfenberg supplied hulls, turrets and the 7.5 cm KwK 40 guns, parts for which were made by Schoeller-Bleckmann in Ternitz, Gusstahl in Judenberg and Klinger in Gumpoldskirchen.

The low delivery by the Nibelungenwerke in November of 1943 was caused by the unsuccessful experiment to increase the ground clearance of the Panzerkampfwagen IV.

During the last war years, the fuel shortage made the use of liquid gas in cylinders necessary for breaking in the tanks. The photograph shows a Ausf. H vehicle with the battery of cylinders mounted on the back.

These two photographs show details of the gas-cylinder battery, which could be put in place quickly.

Between October 1943 and September 1944, the Krupp-Grusonwerk in Magdeburg delivered a total of 1148 Panzerkampfwagen IV and Sturmgeschütz IV, 73 of them in October 1943, 50 in November and 52 in December. As is well known, production at Krupp-Gruson was switched to the Sturmgeschütz IV in December of 1943.

Vomag produced 816 Panzerkampfwagen IV in 1943. The motors came chiefly from Nordbau, Ohrenstein & Koppel in Nordhausen and from MAN. The hulls and turrets were produced in large numbers by Krupp in Essen, Eisenwerke Oberdonau and the Dortmund-Hörder Hüttenverein. The transmissions came mainly from the Zahnradfabrik Friedrichshafen.

Early in 1944 the final version of the Panzerkampfwagen IV (7.5 cm) (Sd.Kfz.161/2), Ausf. J, appeared, mainly manufactured by the Nibelungenwerke. The Ausf.J was produced through the end of the war. While most were completed as tanks with turrets, Ausf. J chassis were also diverted for assembly as Sturmpanzer.

According to H. Techn. V. Blatt 1944 No. 184, dated March 3, 1944, the gasoline-electric auxiliary generator set, starting with the Ausf. J, was no longer installed. At the same time, the traverse mechanism had to be equipped with a second reduction gear, so that the turret could be turned even when the vehicle was in a tilted position. In place of the auxiliary generator set, an additional fuel tank was installed in the engine compartment, its 200 liters increasing the overall fuel capacity to 680 liters. Some of the Schürzen skirts mounted on the Ausf. J were made of a heavy wire mesh. Finally, during the course of production, the exhaust system was also changed. The large muffler was now replaced with two vertical exhaust stacks.

This vehicle's additional filters are easy to see. No need to waste words on the propaganda lettering. In the background is a building of the Nibelungenwerke.

In the course of simplifying the running gear, only three return rollers per side were used instead of the former four. Note that this vehicle, with the last running-gear modifications of the Panzer IV series, uses the earlier idler wheels.

They were modified again in the final series, Ausf. J.

Panzerkampfwagen IV (7.5 cm KwK L/48) Ausf. J (Sd.Kfz.161/2)–the last production version.

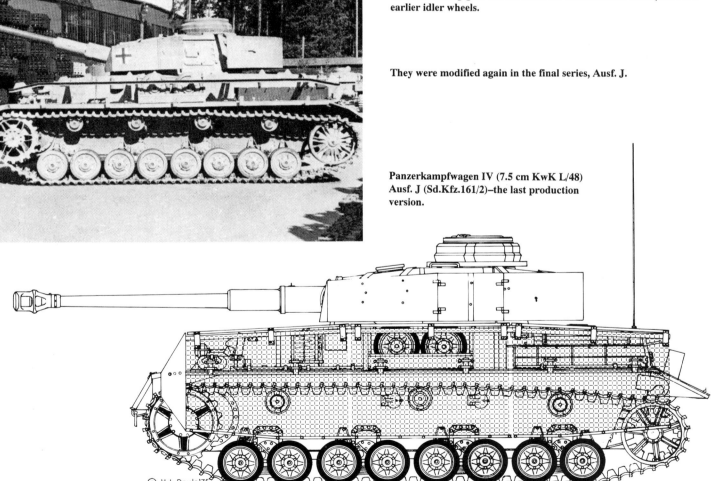

© H.L.Doyle '75

Three views of one of the production vehicles. The exhaust system, in which every bank of cylinders has its own vertical exhaust pipe, is a noteworthy new feature.

A Panzer IV company, obviously on going swimming. The photographs show the new one-piece cover of the commander's cupola that was used on all Ausf. H. ▶▶

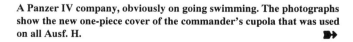

The chassis number of the vehicle could normally be seen on the driver's panel. This is a Panzer IV Ausf. H.

Panzerkampfwagen IV Ausf. H at a training base. The anti-aircraft machine gun mount on the commander's cupola is easy to see. The widespread use of camouflage paste can be seen especially clearly on the vehicle above.

Below: This is how the tanks looked when they were delivered. An MG 34 is mounted on the anti-aircraft mount.

Some of the Panzer IV tanks produced new in 1943 were given a protective covering of Zimmerit, smoke candle launchers attached to the turret, and an improved "Fliegerbeschussgerät 42" [anti-aircraft machine gun mount] attached to the commander's cupola. With the use of "Ostketten" [eastern tracks], the shipping width of the Panzer IV was increased to 3206 mm.

The firm of Rheinmetall-Borsig in Unterlüss was responsible for the production of the 7.5 cm KwK 40 L/48 gun. The Panzer IV was built in this form until the end of the war.

On April 7, 1944 Hitler ordered the final testing and beginning of series production of the new, simplified running gear for the "Einheitsfahrgestell" [uniform chassis] for the Panzer III/IV and Sturmgeschütz to proceed at top speed.

On April 30, 1944 Hitler was impelled by the serious bomb damage to the tank engine and gearbox manufacturing facilities in Friedrichshafen to order that all measures taken for the production, decentralization and security of all armored-vehicle components in short supply, as well as for their contractors, subcontractors and suppliers, be accorded the same level of priority as fighter-plane production. For Sturmgeschütz production, Hitler ordered the same level of priority as the Jäger. According to data from Speer's ministry, the delivery quota for all armored vehicles in 1944 was 40,303 units. In actual fact, by the end of the year only 27,340 units, or 67%, had been completed.

As of July 8, 1944 Hitler ordered that nothing else was to be changed in the basic specifications of the vehicles that were to be produced in the tank program in 1944-45. This was primarily based on the absolute necessity for concentration on producing only three basic entities in terms of the main components, these being:

–the group of 38 (t) vehicles,
–the group of 25-ton vehicles on the Einheitsfahrgestell III/IV, and,
–the group of "Panther" and "Tiger" vehicles.

Above all, this meant that unification of every process of making engines, gearboxes, running gear, power trains, etc. was to be carried out as quickly as possible.

On October 12, 1944 Speer suggested to Hitler that the group of 25-ton vehicles be dropped completely in the process of reducing the number of types to be built. Only the Sturmpanzer based on the Panzer III/IV would continue to be built in the future, and it might well be possible to acquire the needed numbers of units from vehicles being repaired.

Through these measures to limit the number of types, the following goals were to be achieved:

–minimizing of factory susceptibility to crises by minimizing the number of types, thus increasing the number of factories participating in manufacturing one type.

–simplifying the spare-parts supply situation.

–the overburdened vehicles of the 25-ton class would share in the production of like numbers of 38 (t) and Panther vehicles as fully troop-usable vehicles through this transition.

–through the thus possible elimination of HL 120 production, the whole capacity could be converted to production of the air-cooled 12-cylinder Tatra Diesel engine. Thus production of the 38 (t) vehicles in the Reich, and presumably also in the Czech protectorate, could be converted to building this engine.

On May 25, 1944 Hitler judged the armored street-clearing vehicle, developed at the request of Gauleiter Jordan to clear debris caused by air attacks from the streets, to be extraordinarily useful. He requested that, for the time being, ten Panzer III or IV chassis out of repaired stocks be prepared for this purpose.

In 1944 a total of 3554 Panzer IV chassis were reported by the Waffenamt as being completed. The Nibelungenwerke, with an output of about 3274, had turned out the greatest number. On October 17, 1944, a heavy air attack, part of the Allied air offensive against tank manufacturing centers, struck the Nibelungenwerke. On November 4, 1944 Hitler was informed of the severe damage to this factory by means of pictures. The damage to crane equipment as well as the destructive effect of bombs on finished tanks were made particularly clear. Despite the considerable damage, this factory continued to show noteworthy monthly production figures.

The Eisenwerke Oberdonau produced a total of 1797 hulls and 1655 upper bodies for Panzer IV tanks at their assembly facilities in 1944. The Böhler firm in Kapfenberg produced 516 hulls and 695 bodies for Panzer IV from 1941 to 1944.

In 1944, Vomag built only 280 Panzer IV tanks, production having been diverted to the Jagdpanzer IV in early 1944. 75% of the engines came from Nordbau, and the hulls and turrets actually from Witkowitz. As of the summer of 1944, the Auto-Union works in Chemnitz were called on more and more for gearbox production.

In the last war years, the following firms were involved in the production of Maybach HL 120 engines for Panzer IV use: The Maschinenfabrik Bahnbedarf Ohrenstein & Koppel at Nordhausen in the Harz; this factory was set up in 1943 to produce engines of the HL 109 and HL 120 types. From March 1944 to March 1945, 1935 HL 109 and 955 HL 120 engines were built. In June of 1945 the conversion to the air-cooled Tatra 103 12-cylinder engine was supposed to take place.

The firm of Nordbau began to produce the HL 120 engine in February of 1943 and delivered an average of 1000 of these motors per month.

The Nürnberg factory of the MAN firm delivered 2415 HL 120 engines between January 1944 and April 1945.

By the end of March 1945 another 375 Panzerkampfwagen IV had been assembled. In addition, 71 Panzer IV/70(A) were produced.

It is noteworthy that in July of 1944, with Az. 76 g 20 WaPrüf 6/Pz D and contract number SS 4911.0006-2621/43, the Lohner-Werke GmbH of Vienna was hired to build 15 dummies of the Panzerkampfwagen IV that could be dismantled. The price per unit was 1405 Reichsmark. These dummies were obviously intended to conceal German offensive actions.

In 1944 an interesting experiment was made with a rebuilt Pz.Kpfw.IV Ausf. G. The Zahnradfabrik Augsburg built a Panzer IV with hydrostatic drive. This was not a liquid drive, and in fact the gearbox was missing from this test vehicle altogether. The "Thoma" drive was designed so that the primary engine (Maybach HL 120 TRM) was connected directly with two high-performance oil pumps. These oil pumps powered two oil engines. A staggered-

Panzerkampfwagen IV (Ausf. G) rebuilt to test the hydrostatic drive.

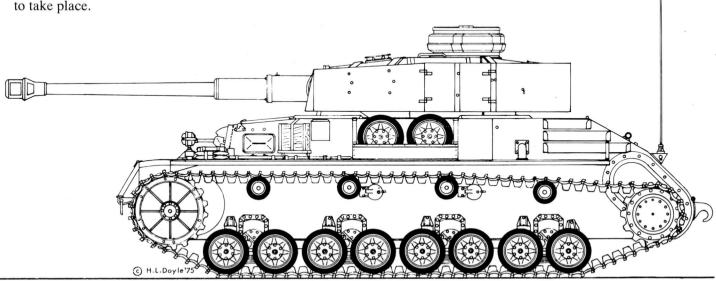

© H.L.Doyle '75

The Zahnradfabrik Augsburg rebuilt a Panzer IV with hydrostatic power. The photographs above show front and rear views of the vehicle, which had its powerplant at the rear. The temporary covering of the powerplant is easy to see.

The photographs at right show the driver's seat and controls; the steering lever was replaced by a wheel.

The engine compartment contained a Maybach HL 120 motor as before. The drive to the oil motor is constructed as a flange. The lateral cutouts for the drive at the rear can be seen clearly.

The hydrostatic motor with the flange to the engine.

plate drive drove the rear drive wheels via transmission gears. The drive wheels had a diameter of about 550 mm, while the idler wheels in front had a diameter of some 780 mm. Power to the hydraulic turret drive was provided simultaneously with the hydrostatic drive.

The drive from the Maybach engine went directly to the drive of the main oil pump.

The inside of the oscillating housing with pressure lines and control vents.

One of the two hydrostatic motors. The control cylinder is visible in the rear aperture.

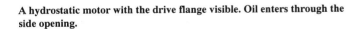

The combined oscillating pumps. The control vent and activation are on the top of the housing. The control piston and cylinder are on the underside of the interior. Pressure lines link the control valve with the piston and cylinder.

A hydrostatic motor with the drive flange visible. Oil enters through the side opening.

The geared oil pump to supply the hydraulic system and activate the control system.

A dismantled hydraulic oscillating motor:

1. Pump housing cover
2. Bearing cup
3. Piston and cylinder plate
4. Cylinder housing
5. Vent cover
6. Pump cylinder housing

A dismantled oil-drive pump:

1. Pump-cylinder housing cover
2. Piston, piston plate and main bearing cup (front)
3. Cylinder housing
4. Vent cover
5. Cylinder housing
6. Pump housing, control cylinder and piston at lower left, oil   inlet and bearing at far left

Test-run results are no longer in existence, and the vehicle was sent to America after the end of the war and subjected to thorough tests by Vickers Inc., Detroit, Michigan. At that time this firm was working on a similar design for an American tank. A report from this firm, dated April 12, 1946, describes the Thoma drive as follows:

The power train consisted of two staggered-plate oil pumps that are assembled as a unit and are driven by a 12-cylinder Maybach engine. Oil is pushed by the pumps to two separate oil engines which power the drive wheels of the tracks. The oil engines are attached to the final drive housings . The engine and power aggregate are located in the rear of the vehicle, and the vehicle is moved by rear-mounted drive wheels. The volume of the pumps is controlled by the driver, who thereby controls the torque of the various pressure conditions that are created by the steering and stopping of the vehicle. In the same manner, the forward and backward movement of the vehicle is achieved by directing the oil flow. Pressurized oil to activate the pumps and engines and for the high-pressure connections was advanced by a geared-wheel pump that was connected to the vehicle's engine by direct drive.

The tests were broken off on account of a lack of spare parts. The vehicle itself is still in the U.S. Army Tank Museum in Aberdeen, Maryland.

Contracts for tanks of the 30-ton class, as replacements for the Panzer IV, were issued as early as 1937 in the name of the Weapons Office to the firms of Daimler-Benz, Henschel, MAN and Porsche. The resulting prototypes of the "VK 3001" vehicle were made obsolete, though, by the appearance of the Russian T 34 tank, just as the "VK 2001" had been by the Panzer III.

A 30-ton tank was planned as a replacement for the Panzer IV and designated "VK 3001", under which designation prototypes were built by various manufacturers. The photograph above shows the "VK 3001 (H)" made by Henschel.

Center: The Porsche firm also developed prototypes in this class and equipped the "VK 3001 (P)" vehicle with a gasoline-electric powerplant.

The bottom photograph shows details of the Porsche vehicle's running gear.

While the designs made by Daimler-Benz and MAN later led to the Panther tank, the prototype vehicles from the Henschel and Porsche firms became the original basis for the later Tiger tank.

In November of 1944, Fried. Krupp AG in Essen undertook conceptual designs for rearming all the German tanks in use by the troops. This resulted in, among other things, a proposal to mount the newly developed Panther turret with its 7.5 cm KwK L/70 gun on a Panzer IV chassis. A wooden model of the long cannon had been previously installed in a normal Panzer IV turret, but enlarging the turret would have been necessary. This in turn could not be carried out because it would have overburdened the chassis.

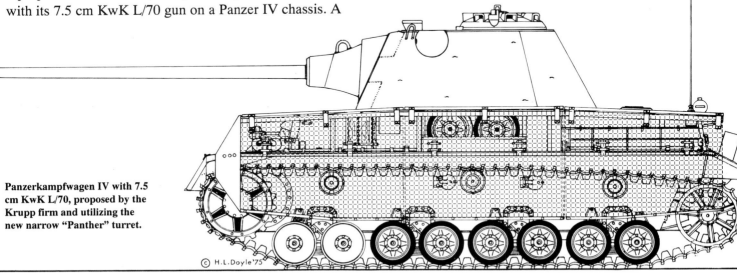

Panzerkampfwagen IV with 7.5 cm KwK L/70, proposed by the Krupp firm and utilizing the new narrow "Panther" turret.

C H.L.Doyle '75

A mockup of this long gun in the original Panzer IV turret.

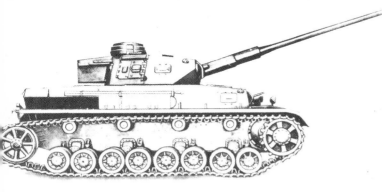

At this point, a reference to the running-gear development of German tanks is appropriate. While the first test and production vehicles had been equipped almost exclusively with coil- or leaf-spring suspension, there appeared in 1936, immediately after E. Kniepkamp took charge of WaPrüf 6, the first designs with torsion-bar suspension. This was preferred since it was less susceptible to shot damage and largely ruled out any blockage of the running gear by ice, snow or mud. In addition, it resulted in an improvement to the running characteristics, chiefly through the possibility of using independent wheel suspension. At that time, such an improvement in handling characteristics was thought to be of no particular value. Despite the obvious advantages, the Krupp engineers stuck with their leaf-spring suspension with road wheels paired in the bogie mounting. As a result, Krupp engineers found themselves in constant opposition to the Heeres Waffenamt.

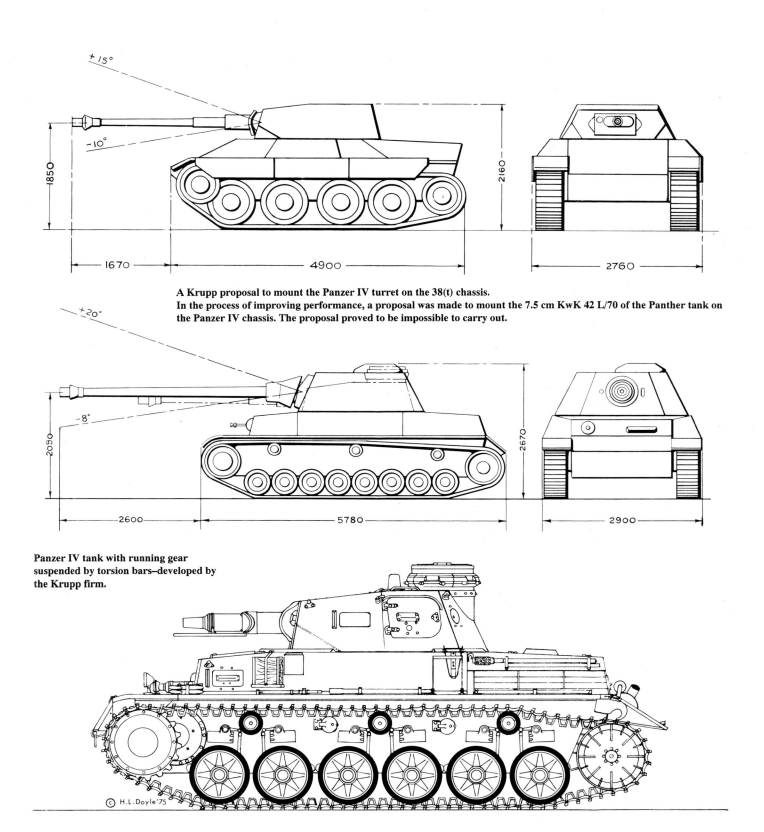

A Krupp proposal to mount the Panzer IV turret on the 38(t) chassis.
In the process of improving performance, a proposal was made to mount the 7.5 cm KwK 42 L/70 of the Panther tank on the Panzer IV chassis. The proposal proved to be impossible to carry out.

Panzer IV tank with running gear suspended by torsion bars—developed by the Krupp firm.

© H.L.Doyle '75

The desire for improved reduction in rubber-tire wear by using larger-diameter road wheels for all fully tracked vehicles also impelled Krupp to develop Panzer IV prototypes with independent wheel suspension on torsion bars and interleaved running gear. One of these prototypes was later used as a "Brückenleger" [bridgelaying] tank. In order to reduce the ground pressure, tests with wider tracks were also conducted.

In 1934 the Heeres Waffenamt had already issued developmental contracts to leading German tire producers for wheel coverings and track pads, for armored vehicles and towing tractors, made of Buna (which did not include any actual rubber). This work was finished as of 1938; during the war, various firms in the occupied territories were also included in this program.

The shortage of rubber as well as the great need for road wheels and return rollers, which quickly wore out, for certain tank types resulted as of 1943 in a redesigning of the road wheels. At this time the Deutsche Eisen-Werke created rubber-saving road wheels that consisted of two strong sheet-steel plates that, between two rubber rings, clamped firmly onto a steel hub under very high pressure. In this way the need for rubber was almost cut in half, and the mechanical vulnerability of the rubber was also strongly reduced. This design, taken freely from the Russian KW I, saved rubber and lengthened the life span of the road wheels and rims. Of course a somewhat higher incidence of track wear had to be taken in the bargain, but there were no complaints about a heightened degree of noise. Tests in Kummersdorf showed an increase of about 10% in wheel resistance.

These rubber-sprung road wheels were introduced on several versions of the Panzer IV whose chassis were overburdened, though not for the entire running gear, but only at the points under the highest pressure. The producers of road wheels for the Panzer III and IV included, among others, the Volkswagenwerk GmbH in Wolfsburg which manufactured some 6000 of these road wheels per month from 1941 to 1944.

In the last months of the war, the final version of the Panzer IV underwent a further simplification of the running gear; instead of the previous four return rollers on each side, only three rollers were used.

A Ausf. X of the Panzer IV was known as Gerät No. 551, but no further information on it is in existence.

In July of 1944 Finland was promised the delivery of ten Panzer IV tanks. In fact, the Finnish Army first bought three test vehicles in 1944, and later in that year it purchased 15 more Panzer IV tanks at a price of 5,000,000 FM apiece. The vehicles were delivered so late that they never saw action during the war. In 1949 and 1950 several Panzer IV tanks were rebuilt as mineclearing vehicles, but they did not prove themselves. From 1951 to 1962, the vehicles were available for training purposes, and the last Panzer IV tanks were mustered out in September of 1962. The vehicles were not very popular among the Finnish Army. Above all, problems with the suspension and steering were cited.

As early as May of 1942, Hungary had obtained 22 Panzer IV tanks with short guns for its army, and another ten units followed in September of that year. Additional Panzer IV tanks were sent there in the last months of the year.

Between March and September of 1942, Romania had obtained eleven Panzer IV tanks. In 1943 and 1944 about 88 Panzer IV tanks with long guns were delivered to Bulgaria. Romania also received a similar number of these vehicles. After August 23, 1944 Romania equipped its armored units, now used to fight against the German Wehrmacht, with the Panzer IV tanks that remained in the country.

Some Panzer IV were also delivered to Croatia.

The Red Army used captured Panzer IV tanks only in limited numbers and later turned them over to units of the "National Committee for Free Germany."

In North Africa, units of the "Free Polish Forces" used Panzer IV tanks for training purposes. From there, they and other mar materials made their way to Syria and Jordan, where they remained in service for years side by side with Russian and British equipment. In the Near Eastern War of 1967, the Arab forces were still using Panzer IV tanks.

Panzerkampfwagen IV (7.5 cm) Ausf. A (Vs.Kfz.622)

Panzerkampfwagen IV (7.5 cm) Ausf. E (Sd.Kfz.161)

Panzerkampfwagen IV (7.5 cm) Ausf. E (Sd.Kfz.161)

Panzerkampfwagen IV (7.5 cm) Ausf. F1 (Sd.Kfz.161)

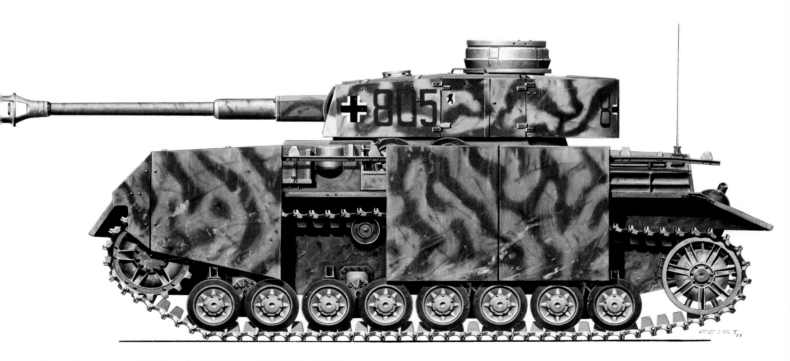

Panzerkampfwagen IV (7.5 cm KwK L/48) Ausf. J (Sd.Kfz.161/2)

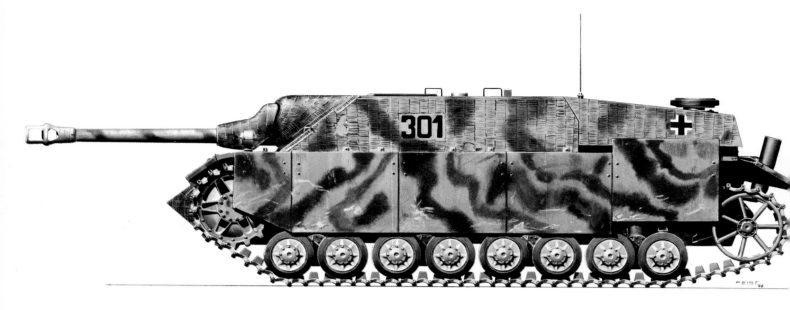

Jagdpanzer IV Ausf. F (Sd.Kfz.162)

15 cm sFH 18/1 auf Fgst. Panzerkampfwagen III/IV (Sf) (Sd.Kfz.165) "Hummel"

Limited numbers of Panzer IV vehicles were also supplied to allies of the Reich and neutral countries. This photograph shows a Panzer IV with a Croatian crew.

In the last war years, Spain received a number of Panzerkampfwagen IV Ausf. H, which remained in use by the troops there for years.

The Finnish Army continued to use Panzer IV tanks for many years after the war ended. One of these vehicles is on display at the Finnish Army Museum.

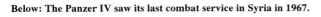
Below: The Panzer IV saw its last combat service in Syria in 1967.

As usual, supply difficulties, particularly of spare parts, soon reduced captured vehicles to temporary utilization.

For political reasons, German armored vehicles were also delivered to neutral countries during the war. For example, Turkey received Panzer IV tanks of the newest type in early 1943. In 1943 a number of brand-new Panzer IV tanks were delivered to Spain, and were still being used by the troops in the nineteen-fifties.

In 1950 a Panzerkampfwagen IV Ausf. G, which had been kept at the British Tank Museum, was returned to Germany as a gift to the Bundeswehr. The tank is still at the Panzer Museum in Munster. The well-known tank museums of various countries include a number of Panzer IV vehicles in their inventories.

Summation of Panzerkampfwagen IV Production

1937   13 Stück von Krupp-Gruson ab Oktober
1938   102 Stück von Krupp-Gruson
1939   141 Stück Panzer IV von Krupp-Gruson
       6 Stück Fahrgestelle für Brückenleger im August
       6 Stück Fahrgestelle für Brückenleger im September
1940   278 Stück Panzer IV von Krupp-Gruson
       2 Stück Fahrgestelle an WaPrüf. 4 für Sfl IVa im Februar
       10 Stück Fahrgestelle für Brückenleger an WaPrüf. 5 im April. Im Februar wurden zwei der für Brückenleger freigegebenen Fahrgestelle der Ausf. C für den Aufbau von Inf. Sturmsteg Fahrzeugen verwendet.
1941   437 Stück Panzer IV von Krupp-Gruson
       1 Stück Panzer IV mit 5 cm KwK 39 L/60 von Krupp-Gruson
       40 Stück Panzer IV von Vomag
       3 Stück Panzer IV von Ni-Werke

1942   88 Stück Panzer IV (7,5 cm L/24) von Krupp-Gruson
       482 Stück Panzer IV (7,5 cm L/43) von Krupp-Gruson
       25 Stück Panzer IV (7,5 cm L/24) von Vomag
       212 Stück Panzer IV (7,5 cm L/43) von Vomag
       11 Stück Panzer IV (7,5 cm L/24) von Ni-Werke
       176 Stück Panzer IV (7,5 cm L/43) von Ni-Werke
       1 Stück Fahrgestell für Prototyp Panzer III/IV von Vomag
1943   821 Stück Panzer IV von Krupp-Gruson
       817 Stück Panzer IV von Vomag (davon einer nicht verwendbar)
       1376 Stück Panzer IV von Ni-Werke
       10 Stück Fahrgestelle für Sturmpanzer von Ni-Werke
       30 Stück Fahrgestelle für Sturmgeschütz IV von Ni-Werke
1944   280 Stück Panzer IV von Vomag
       2845 Stück Panzer IV von Ni-Werke
       258 Stück Fahrgestelle für Sturmpanzer von Ni-Werke
       207 Stück Fahrgestelle für Panzer IV/70 (A) von Ni-Werke
1945   375 Stück Panzer IV von Ni-Werke
       71 Stück Panzer IV/70 (A) von Ni-Werke
       9124

	Krupp	Vomag	Ni-Werke	Insgesamt
1937	13	–	–	13
1938	102	–	–	102
1939	153	–	–	153, davon 12 Fgst. für BL.
1940	290	–	–	290, davon 2 Fgst. für Sfl IVa, 10 Fgst. für BL.
1941	438	40	3	481, davon 1 mit 5 cm KwK L/60
1942	570	237 − 1	187	995, davon 1 Prototyp für Gw III/IV
1943	821	817	1376 + 40 Fgst.	3054, davon 10 Fgst. für StuPz., 30 Fgst. für StuG IV
1944	–	280	2845 + 465 Fgst.	3590, davon 258 Fgst. für StuPz., 207 Pz.IV/70
1945	–	–	375 + 71 Fgst.	446, davon 71 Pz. IV/70 (A)
				9124

	1937	1938	1939	1940	1941	1942	1943	1944	1945	Insgesamt
Panzerkampfwagen IV (7,5 cm L/24)	13	102	141	278	480	124	–	–	–	1138
Panzerkampfwagen IV (7,5 cm L/43/48)	–	–	–	–	–	870	3014	3125	375	7384
Panzerkampfwagen IV (5 cm L/60)	–	–	–	–	1	–	–	–	–	1
Panzerkampfwagen IV/70 (A)	–	–	–	–	–	–	–	207	71	278
Fahrgestell für Brückenleger	–	–	10	10	–	–	–	–	–	20
Fahrgestell für Inf. Sturmsteg	–	–	2	–	–	–	–	–	–	2
Fahrgestell für Sfl IVa	–	–	–	2	–	–	–	–	–	2
Fahrgestell für Prototyp III/IV	–	–	–	–	–	1	–	–	–	1
Fahrgestell für Sturmpanzer IV	–	–	–	–	–	–	10	258	–	268
Fahrgestell für Sturmgeschütz IV	–	–	–	–	–	–	30	–	–	30
										9124

Panzerjäger Vehicles

The chassis of the Panzer IV, proven and available in large numbers, formed the basis for a number of variants, many of which were to be found among German troop units until the war's end.

At a conference with Hitler at the Berghof on May 26, 1941 it was decided to create a self-propelled carriage for the 10.5 cm cannon as well as one for the 12.8 cm gun. The two vehicles were to be used not only for action against bunkers, but also to defend against the heavy tanks that could be expected from Britain and later from America. The necessity of defense against Russian tanks was not even mentioned in this report.

The 10.5 cm high-performance cannon had been developed by the Krupp firm and completed in 1941. This weapon, known as the 10.5 cm K 18, had a barrel length of 5460 mm, or L/52. The muzzle velocity of the armor-piercing shell was 835 meters per second, and the shell weight was 15.6 kg. The total weight of the weapon, including the double-action muzzle brake, was 1962 kg. It was mounted in a lightly armored superstructure, with a limited traverse, on a Panzer IV chassis. The fighting compartment was open at the rear. The vehicle's official

10.5 cm K 18 auf Panzer-Selbstfahrlafette IVa

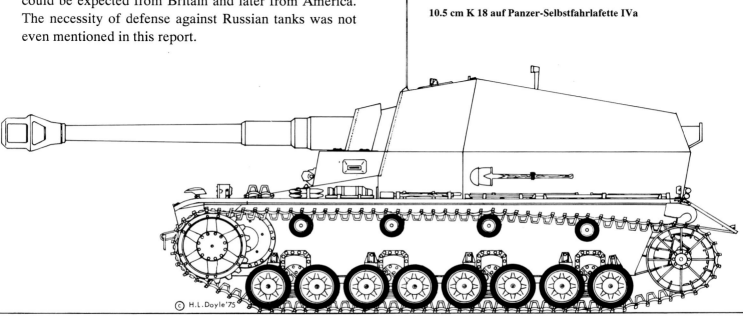

A cross-section drawing of the 10.5 cm gun for self-propelled vehicles.

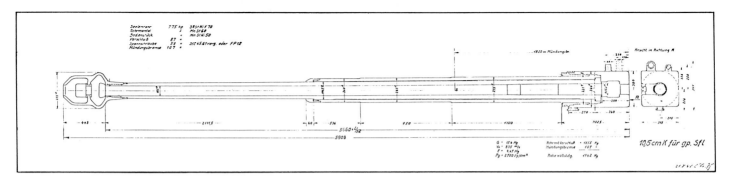

designation was "10.5 cm K 18 auf Panzer-Selbstfahrlafette IVa." There were only two prototypes completed, one of which was shown to Hitler on March 31, 1941. As for the need for this vehicle, communications with the AHA were opened, in view of the fact that series production could not be counted on before the spring of 1942.

In this way a weapon would have become available that would have been able to knock out any Russian tank at any range. Once again the bureaucrats of the Waffenamt made such a solution impossible. Only the two prototypes were ever built. General Munzel, in his book "Die deutschen gepanzerten Truppen bis 1945", gives the only indication to date as to the use of these two vehicles. They were originally turned over to Panzerjäger Abteilung 521 and were to be used in the planned attack on Gibraltar. At the beginning of the Russian campaign they were turned over to the 3.Panzer-Division. The vehicles proved to be sufficient in front, but they were only lightly armored on the sides and in the rear. In addition, their mobility left something to be desired, as the vehicle was overloaded by the installation of the heavy gun. One of the vehicles was destroyed when its ammunition exploded; the other was sent back to Germany in October of 1941 after it had fought successfully against numerous Russian T 34 tanks. No further attempts to utilize this weapon are known.

Under the influence of the heavy fighting around Stalingrad, new minimum requirements for assault weapons were established in September of 1942. Armor strengths of 100 mm in front and 40 to 50 mm on the sides were suggested. The ground clearance was to be 50 cm. Wider tracks and the lowest possible firing height were called for. The long 7.5 cm KwK L/70 was to be used as the primary weapon. With a top speed of 25 km/hr, the overall weight was to increase to some 26 tons without causing any concern. While a fully new chassis was planned at first, it was necessary on the basis of war events to make use of Panzer IV chassis, already available and being produced in

Krupp created one of the prototypes of self-propelled Panzerjäger with a 10.5 cm gun. These photographs show three views of this vehicle, of which only two specimens were built.

large numbers. Gerät No. 820 was a Sturmgeschütz III superstructure fitted to a Panzerkampfwagen IV chassis. Gerät No. 822 was a Sturmgeschütz 43 on Panzer IV chassis with a 7.5 cm L/70 gun made by Alkett, and Gerät No. 823 was a Sturmhaubitze 43 on Panzer IV chassis with a 10.5 cm StuH 42/4 howitzer, also made by Alkett.

At this time, attempts were made to increase Sturmgeschütz production by all means until the transition to the new vehicle could take place. Among other things, attempts were made to give the previous chassis some of the required characteristics of the new Sturmgeschütz. The idea was chiefly to increase the ground clearance and use wider tracks. Attempts were also made to determine whether, after the transition from Panzer III to Panther production and the new Panther production capacity, the eventual Sturmgeschütz might be mounted on the Panzer IV chassis, so as to make direct use of its production capacity.

Hitler welcomed the suggestion that the ground clearance of the Sturmgeschütz be increased to 50 cm quickly by using new box-type running gear. At the same time, widening the tracks was supposed to decrease the ground pressure from about 1 kg per square cm to 0.7 kilogram per centimeter squared.

But since such a transition could not, on the basis of existing capacities, be possible before May of 1943, the question was raised again of whether it might be possible to achieve the other characteristics of the modified Sturmgeschütz by this date too. The main goals were the long 7.5 cm gun, front armor increased to 100 mm, and angled surfaces. Again the expedited use of the Panzer IV chassis was considered, and the same engine and gearbox as before were to be used.

If a new design should nevertheless become necessary for the Sturmgeschütz, then heavy chassis that could carry the long 8.8 cm cannon were to be given priority.

Alkett thereupon developed the Gerät No. 822, a Sturmgeschütz based on the Panzer IV, with the 7.5 cm L/70 gun, and as a parallel type, Gerät No. 823, which carried the 10.5 cm Sturmhaubitze in the same body.

In October of 1942 the model of an Sturmgeschütz on a Panzer IV chassis was displayed. Hitler's final request was thereupon made, calling for the creation of an Sturmgeschütz with the chassis, engine and gearbox of the Panzer IV, the 7.5 cm L/70 gun, angled surfaces, 50 cm ground clearance and wider tracks.

In December of 1942 instructions were given to rearm the Sturmgeschütz quickly with the 7.5 cm L/70 in place of the 7.5 cm L/48 caliber gun. To do this, appropriate plans were to be made and supplied involving the comparative use of Panzer III, Panzer IV and Leopard components. In this respect, Speer called attention to the fact that it was not possible for industry to take on a complete conversion twice in one year without considerable interruptions in Sturmgeschütz production. The change to the light 7.5 cm Kanone L/70 could only be made in 1943 in terms of production technology if the transition was that to the final version of the Sturmgeschütz.

The wooden model of the new leichte Panzerjäger was displayed in May of 1943 and approved by Hitler. This very well-made wooden model of the Panzerjäger was designed by Vomag. Its overall height of some 1700 mm reached the limit of what could be carried practically cross-country. The exhibition of the soft steel prototype of the leichte Panzerjäger with 7.5 cm L/48 gun on Panzer IV chassis took place on October 20, 1943. Production began immediately thereafter. The armor plate was produced by the Witkowitzer Bergbau- und Eisenhütten-Gewerkschaft. In the "O-Series" of this vehicle, the superstructure front plate had rounded edges, but a straight superstructure front plate was used on the series-production vehicle. The manufacturers of the primary armament (7.5 cm Pak 39 L/48) were the firms of Rheinmetall-Borsig in Unterlüss and the Seitz-Werke in Kreuznach. The vehicles, which first saw service at the beginning of 1944, were designated "Jagdpanzer IV, Ausf. F" (Sd.Kfz.162).

The following differences from the normal Panzer IV chassis existed:

The bow of the hull, made of 50 mm armor plate, came to a sharp angle, the emergency escape hatch was rectangular and fitted with a new lock. Instead of the auxiliary generator set used in the Panzer IV, there was an additional fuel tank, and the filler caps for the tanks had been relo-

The "0-Serie" Jagdpanzer IV had the curved superstructure front plate. The conical covers on the front protect the ports for firing the machine guns from inside the vehicle.

Upper Right: Vomag designed a "leichter Panzerjäger auf Panzer IV Fahrgestell", a wooden mockup of which is shown here. The chassis was unchanged from that of the Panzer IV. The low overall profile of the vehicle is especially striking.

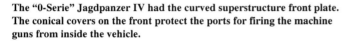

Side and rear views of the "Jagdpanzer IV, Ausf. F (Sd.Kfz.162)."

The vehicles could be used with or without muzzle brakes. This photograph shows one of the vehicles in action. The maintenance hatches for the steering brakes were opened for better ventilation during long marches.

The production version of the "leichter Panzerjäger" was fitted with a straight front plate which was no longer curved at the sides. The interlocked edges of the plates can be seen clearly at the welding seams. Details of the "Saukopf" gun mantle are also visible.

A rear view of the vehicle shows details of the running gear, including the steel tired return rollers.

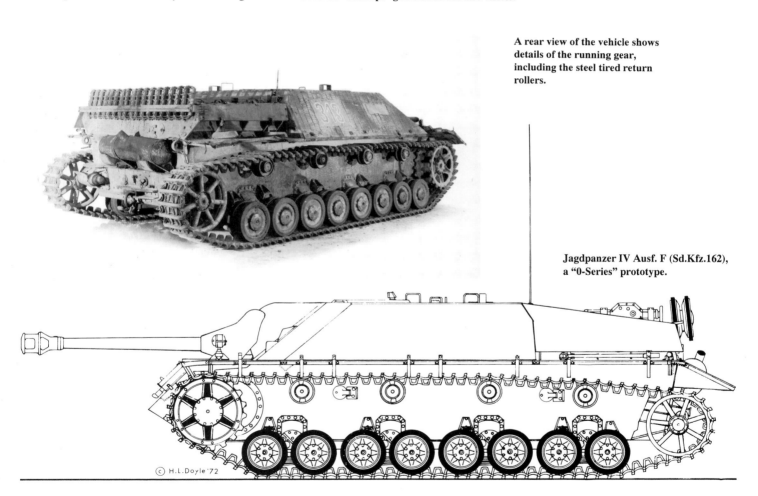

Jagdpanzer IV Ausf. F (Sd.Kfz.162), a "0-Series" prototype.

© H.L.Doyle '72

cated. So had the arrangement of the brake-cooling vents, the fighting-compartment heating and the radio equipment and its attachments. Additional Schürzen side skirts had been attached, as on most vehicles of the time. The fighting weight amounted to 24 tons with a four-man crew and 79 7.5 cm shells aboard. The chassis type used was the Type 7/BW. The firing height was 1400 mm, the overall height 1860 mm. In the vehicles used by platoon, company and unit commanders the four men of the regular crew were joined by a fifth, a radio operator. He operated a machine gun that protruded through an opening in the superstructure front plate. When not in use, this machine gun port was protected by a conical armor cover.

In all, 769 of these vehicles were completed in 1944.

It should also be noted that the eight 10.5 cm le.F.H. auf Sfl.IVb [light field howitzers on self-propelled IV b chassis] (Geschützwagen IV b) built in November of 1942 were also supposed to a field unit.

At a conference at the Führer's headquarters in December of 1943, Hitler welcomed the suggestion to make up for the loss of Sturmgeschütz production capacity by quickly devising a superstructure for the Panzer IV out of components of the superstructure formerly used for the Sturmgeschütz on the Panzer III chassis. In this suggestion he saw the possibility of utilizing this vehicle in Panzer units and thus simplifying supply of spare-parts. Hitler also wished the first model of the Sturmgeschütz with the modified superstructure on the Panzer IV chassis to be displayed as soon as its firing tests were finished. This display was planned for December 16, 1943.

On the occasion of this exhibition, at which the Panzerjäger IV and the "instant solution" of the Sturmgeschütz on the Panzer IV chassis were shown, the leichte Panzerjäger attracted particular attention because of its extraordinarily low body and its smooth lines. The Sturmgeschütz on the Panzer IV chassis met with Hitler's approval.

The chassis construction and assembly of these vehicles took place at the Krupp-Gruson AG in Magdeburg-Buckau. The hulls were delivered by the firms of Böhler in Kapfenberg, Eisenwerke Oberdonau in Linz, Krupp in Essen and EHW in Bochum. The armor components for the superstructure were made by the Brandenburgische Eisenwerke. With front armor of 80 mm and side armor plates of 30 mm, the fighting weight was 23 tons. The crew, as usual with Sturmgeschütz, numbered four men. The ammunition load was 63 rounds. The 7.5 cm StuK 40 L/48 guns were delivered by the firms of Wimag in Berlin and Skoda in Pilsen.

These "Sturmgeschütz IV" saw service at the front along with the Sturmgeschütz III, and were also used to equip some of the III.Abteilungen (third battalions) in several Panzer Regiments.

Efforts were supposed to be made to balance the resulting interruption in Sturmgeschütz production by giving the greatest support to reestablishing full production quickly. The quotas set were 350 units to be built in December and 500 in January 1944, including Sturmgeschütz III, Panzerjäger (made by Vomag), and Sturmgeschütz IV (by Krupp-Gruson).

The Krupp-Gruson AG had begun to build these vehicles in December of 1943, after production of the Panzerkampfwagen IV had ended there in the same month. In 1944 a total of 1006 Sturmgeschütz IV units were completed, followed by another 102 by March 1945. Thus the total production numbered 1138 units.

On December 17, 1943, the machine gun with all-around fire, installed on a armored vehicle and operated from under cover, was first shown and gained Hitler's complete approval. It was to be made available to the troops at once in as great quantities as possible, and preparations were to be made for its installation in all Sturmgeschütz and Panzerjäger that as yet had no machine guns.

The display of new army equipment on January 26, 1944 showed that, within the parameters of technical installation and delivery potential, the new-type 7.5 cm L/70 gun was to be installed in the Vomag Panzerjäger and the "Sturmgeschütz neuer Art" (new design).

Because of expectations of remarkable results from rigid mounted guns in the Sturmgeschütz and Panzerjäger, Hitler requested on January 28, 1944 that the tests then

From 1944 on, Krupp-Gruson produced only the "Sturmgeschütz IV", a vehicle composed of the "Sturmgeschütz 40" superstructure on the Panzer IV chassis. This photograph shows the machine gun in a folding shield at the loader's position.

A comparison of the two Sturmgeschütz, with the Panzer IV chassis in the foreground, with its unique driver's compartment.

Sturmgeschütz IV

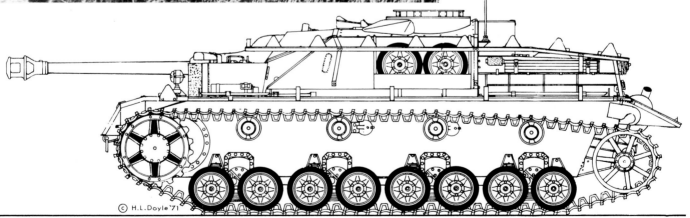

© H.L.Doyle '71

These Sturmgeschütz IV, built until the war ended, were later equipped with a "Rundum-Feuer" machine gun mount for all-around fire, operated from inside the fighting compartment.

underway be speeded up, so as to arrive as soon as possible at a clear awareness of any resulting disadvantages.

On March 15, 1944 Hitler was informed through photographs and statistics of the results to date of firing tests with the shortened recoil. These tests were to have full support because of their importance, especially because of the added significance of a comparison between the angled firing at a 90-degree angle to the vertical mounting of the Rundumfeuer-MG [all-around machine gun] in an armored vehicle. At the beginning of April 1944, Hitler again requested the accelerated delivery of the Rundumfeuer-MG for the Sturmgeschütz, so that it could be available in large numbers for practical testing by the troops. At the end of May 1944 the first positive evaluations of the Rundumfeuer-MG from three Sturmgeschütz units finally reached him.

Early in April 1944 Hitler was given the first photographs of the Vomag Panzerjäger with the 7.5 cm L/70 gun installed. He considered this development to be one of the most important of the time. He asked that these vehicles be displayed as soon as possible, and also wanted to see the following vehicles on April 20, 1944:

–the old Sturmgeschütz auf Panzer III
–the old Sturmgeschütz auf Panzer IV

–the Vomag Panzerjäger mit 7.5 cm L/48 gun
–the Vomag Panzerjäger mit 7.5 cm L/70 gun

As a result of this display, at which the Panzerjäger 38 (t) was also shown, the latter and the Vomag Panzerjäger L/70 were chosen for priority production, with a requested quota of 1000 and 800 units per month respectively.

In July of 1944 Hitler ordered that in its final state, the

This photograph shows the "Rundum-Feuer" machine gun on the roof of the Sturmgeschütz. The loading hatch on the side is easy to see.

A cutaway view of the fighting compartment , showing the installation of this machine gun mount in the "Hetzer." It was installed identically in the Sturmgeschütz IV.

whole Panzer IV production was to be converted to the "Sturmgeschütz auf Einheitsfahrgestell III/IV" with the long L/70 gun. Since on the one hand the existing production potential did not allow such measures to be taken quickly, and on the other it was necessary to get the new gun to the front quickly in as great quantities as possible, Hitler gave his approval to the following transitional guidelines:

–As of August 1944, an additional 50 units, in excess of the expected quota of 300 Panzer IV tanks, were to be produced with the superstructure designed by ALKETT mounting the long L/70 gun. Because of the urgent need for newly created divisions, the production of these vehicles should be moved ahead to the first half of August. (Nibelungenwerk in St. Valentin used superstructures mounting the long 7,5 cm gun, whose design had been modified by ALKETT from the Jagdpanzer IV superstructure. Designated as the "Panzer IV/70 (A)", 278 units were produced in the period from August 1944 to March 1945.)

–As of September 1944, through appropriate further intervention into the Panzer IV production quota, at least 100 of these vehicles were supposed to be produced.

–By October 1944 at the latest, the possibility was to be created through appropriate conversions by the armor

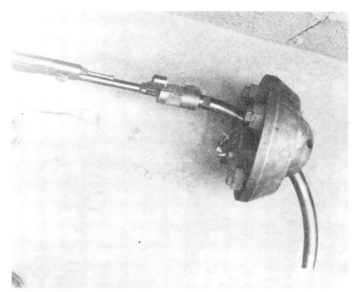

This photograph shows the roof of a Panzerjäger IV with the attachments for a periscope.

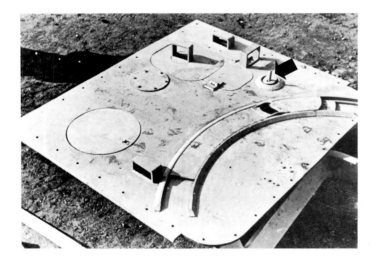

For defense in close combat, the MP 43 and 44 were proposed as of 1944 with a curved attachment for installation in armored vehicles. Since the weapon could be turned 360 degrees on this attachment, in principle, all dead angles of the vehicle were eliminated.

manufacturers to make it possible to produce at least fifty more vehicles with the long gun. After this, the transitional vehicle (Panzer IV/70 (A)) was no longer to be produced, but instead, production was to be transferred to assembling additional Vomag Panzerjäger with the long gun.

—In the continuing production program, after October, production was to be converted from the Panzer IV tank to the Vomag Panzerjäger at a rate of an additional 50 per month. The conversion of the entire production capacity of 350 Panzer IV from tanks to Panzerjäger was to be concluded at the latest by February 1945.

Beginning in August 1944, Vomag produced a total of 930 Panzer IV/70 (V) (Sd. Kfz. 162/1). This vehicle, weighing 25.8 tons, likewise had a four- or five-man crew and was the equal of any enemy tanks thanks to its considerably increased firepower. These Jagdpanzer vehicles, known in front-line slang as "Guderian ducks", unfortunately proved to be front heavy due to the heavy frontal armor and long gun and were hard to steer in rough country. The simplifications to the Panzer IV chassis also appeared in this vehicle, with only three return rollers being installed on each side in later lots. The front road wheels were also of the steel-wheel type in order to prevent damage to rubber tired road wheels.

The desire to install the long 7.5 cm 42 L/70 gun in the Jagdpanzer IV resulted in this prototype, which again used an unchanged Panzer IV chassis.

Panzer IV/70 (A), an interim solution

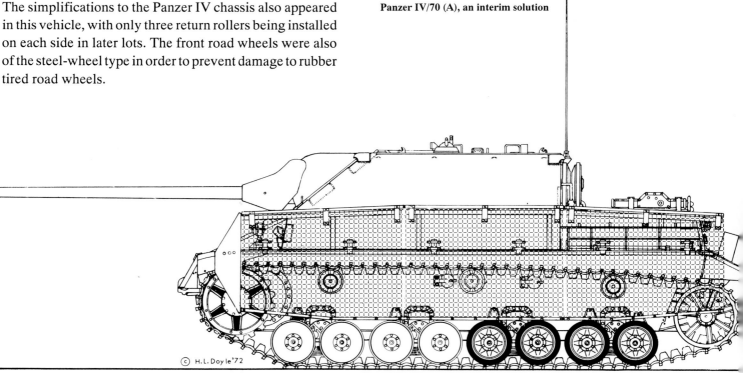

© H.L.Doyle'72

As a so-called interim solution, the Nibelungenwerke installed the long gun in a raised superstructure. This photograph shows a row of chassis intended for this purpose, the last four of them already equipped with the higher superstructure. The chassis in front has only three return rollers.

The vehicles before the guns were installed. The first vehicles were delivered at the end of 1944.

The finished vehicle of this type with the 7.5 cm Pak 42 L/70 installed. To the right of this gun is the port for firing a machine-gun from inside.

The final vehicle in the development of the Jagdpanzer IV was the "Panzer IV/70 (V)." One of the first production models is shown with and without Schürzen skirts. The unchanged Panzer IV running gear is still in use.

The long gun rested on an external travel lock. With this gun, the vehicles were equal to all enemy tanks, but their chassis had reached the end of their potential.

Panzer IV/70 (V) (Sd.Kfz.162/1)

© H.L. Doyle '72

It soon became obvious that these vehicles, heavily overloaded at the front, had to be equipped partially with steel road wheels. The first two road wheels of this vehicle are of the new type. The running gear also includes only three return rollers.

Manufacture of the armored components were by the same firms that had already produced the L/48 version. The 7.5 cm Pak 42 L/70 was built by the Gustloff-Werke in Weimar and Skoda in Pilsen. The vehicles reached the Panzerjäger Abteilungen of the Panzer Divisions in small numbers until the war ended. It must still be added that Generaloberst Guderian was not convinced of the value of this Sturmgeschütz L/70 in 1943. He authorized a further investigation of the necessity of this development and, if justified, the abandonment of the vehicles. To him, the Sturmgeschütz with the 7.5 cm StuK 40 was sufficient for all tasks.

In 1944 a total of 1530 of the Jagdpanzer IV with the 7.5 cm Pak 39 L/48 and Panzer IV/70 (V) with the L/70 gun were produced by Vomag. In the first three months of 1945, Vomag turned out another 370 Panzer IV/70 (V).

Finally, an attempt was made by the Fried.Krupp AG to mount the 8.8 cm Pak 43/3 L/71 on the Panzer IV chassis, at least on paper. In the Krupp version of November 17, 1944, though, the carrying capacity of the chassis must have been exceeded greatly. The "Panzerjäger IV mit 8.8 cm Pak 43/3 L/71" remained a project.

Still to be noted in this respect are the attempts to mount the recoilless 7.5 cm Panzerwurfkanone in a turret on a Panzer IV chassis. The wooden mockups showed various arrangements of the weapons, with the installation of an indicator gun (ranging gun) being of interest. The turret design had openings in the rear in order to safely exhaust the backflash of the gun.

Recoilless tank guns were proposed, mounted in a turret on a Panzer IV chassis. These photographs show front and side views of a wooden model of this proposal.

A Krupp proposal for the installation of the 8.8 cm Pak 43/3 in the Panzerjäger IV. This version could not be built.

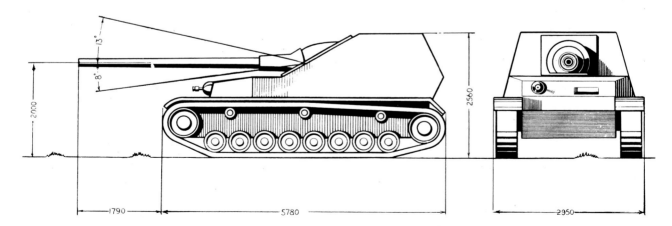

Sturmpanzer

In a document dated June 9, 1941 (No. 548/41 gKdos), the question was raised of to what extent it would be possible to put a weapon of 15 cm (heavy infantry gun) caliber with a high shrapnel effect in the field. The expedient solutions on Panzer I, II and III chassis that had been made for several years had not been able to meet these requirements.

On October 14, 1942, Hitler was shown the designs, submitted by ALKETT, of a Sturmpanzer with a special heavy infantry gun on the Panzer IV chassis. He requested prompt information as to the date by which some 40 to 60 units of such a vehicle could be produced, taking into consideration the new design of the gun needed for it. If it should be possible to produce a definite number of this Sturm-Infanterie-Geschütz as early as the spring of 1943, then the need for such quantities of a Sturmpanzer on the Porsche Tiger chassis would no longer exist.

In order to heighten the effect of the 15 cm sIG [heavy infantry gun] shell for action against buildings, Hitler stressed the need for a thin-walled shell with a high explosive effect.

At the same time, Hitler again requested a design of a 21 or 22 cm mortar in a Sturmpanzer. Attempts were to be made to mount a superstructure, with 80 mm front armor, on the Panzer IV chassis. The barrel could possibly be shortened, as the gun would be used exclusively as a sort of mine launcher. For this gun, a shell with an effect like that of a mine was to be developed at once. The shot range was not to be more than four kilometers.

On February 7, 1943, after model photos of the new 15 cm Sturmpanzer with 100 mm front armor had been submitted, Hitler expected the first vehicles of the 40-piece series, scheduled for completion by May 12, to be completed as soon as possible. After that a further 20 units were to be built.

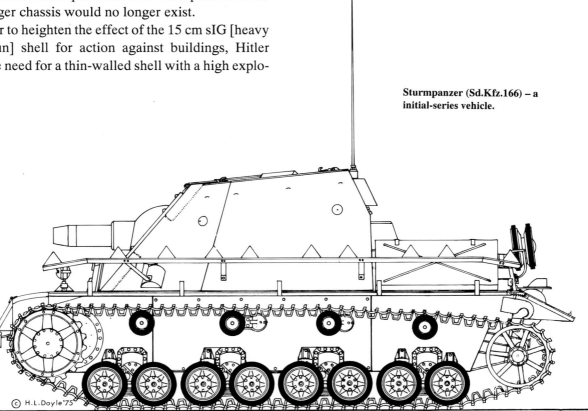

Sturmpanzer (Sd.Kfz.166) – a initial-series vehicle.

The first series of "Sturmpanzer" were made mounting superstructures on repaired tank chassis that had been returned for major overhaul. These photographs show one of the first series still using the "Fahrersehklappe 80" of the Tiger I tank. The red registration plates were only used during testing. As a rule, armored full-track vehicles of the German Wehrmacht carried no license plates.

In an unofficial list, this vehicle appeared as "Gerät 581–Sturmpanzerwagen 604/16" (ALKETT sIG auf Panzer IV with hanging mount).

In April of 1943 there was a special action in which the first vehicles of the "Sturmpanzer (Sd.Kfz.166)" were assembled. For this purpose, the Nibelungenwerk delivered 20 repaired chassis in April and 32 more in May. The Eisenwerke Oberdonau produced superstructures for these vehicles. Assembly took place at the motor vehicle workshop in Vienna, under the cooperation of the Austrian Saurer Works and Simmering-Graz-Pauker. As early as May 4, 1943 Speer was to convey Hitler's thanks to the Heeres Zeugamt Wien [Army Ordnance Depot in Vienna] for outstanding achievement in the production of the "Sturmpanzer."

Hitler decided on April 14, 1943 that the Sturmpanzer units were to be turned over to Generaloberst Guderian for training. Of the planned sixty vehicles, fifty were to be utilized at the front, while the rest were to be reserved for a special action to be ordered by Hitler.

On May 4, 1943 Hitler said he was convinced that an extraordinary need would arise as soon as the Sturmpanzer reached the troops. He asked that the possibility of constantly taking chassis of Panzer IV tanks sent home for repair and fitting them with this gun be investigated. Plans were to be made to determine the shortest possible time involved and the number of units that could be produced per month.

At the same time, Hitler chose the name "Sturmpanzer" for the vehicle on Panzer IV chassis with the new Skoda 15 cm heavy infantry gun, to differentiate it from the Sturmhaubitze with the 10.5 cm light field howitzer.

Since the designation of armored vehicles constantly led to confusion, Hitler requested a list with clear concepts for the naming of all Panzerkampfwagen [tanks], Panzer-Jäger [tank destroyers], Sturmgeschütz [assault guns], Sturmhaubitze [assault howitzers], Sturmpanzer [assault tanks] and Selbstfahrlafetten [self-propelled guns].

On May 15, 1943 Hitler was shown the original model of the "Sturmpanzer", which won his approval.

After the first series of 52 vehicles was delivered, it soon became obvious that the vehicles, with an ammunition load of 38 shells, a five-man crew and a fighting weight of 28.2 tons, were heavily overloaded. On January 28 Hitler agreed to the suggestion that, because of overloading of the chassis then in use, Sturmpanzer production would cease after the current series of 60 units was finished until the new chassis had proved itself. In the meantime, corresponding numbers of Panzer IV tanks were to be produced instead of the Sturmpanzer. In spite of this, it was possible in December of 1943 to resume production at the rate of ten vehicles. At first the road wheels on the front bogie were replaced with rubber-sprung steel wheels, and when this measure turned out to be insufficient, the second pair of road wheels on the second bogie from the front was also replaced with these steel tired road wheels.

Sturmpanzer (Sd.Kfz.166) – one of the last series.

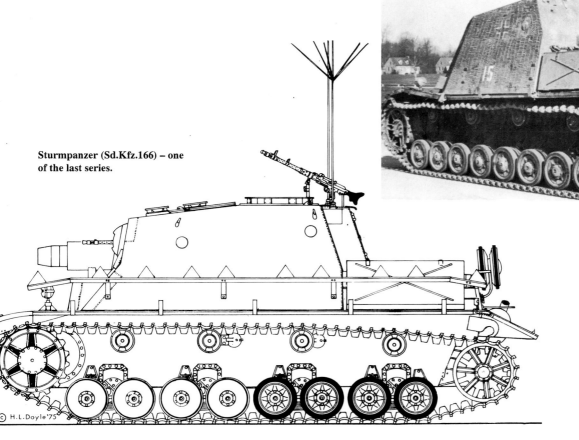

In this version, the driver's visor was replaced by an angled periscope. These photographs show the front and rear of the Sturmpanzer (Sd.Kfz.166) with Zimmerit applied.

In the final version, a ball mount was also installed above the driver's position for engaging soft targets. This photograph shows a command vehicle with added radio and antenna equipment.

The gun mount was transported in a similar way to the barrel.

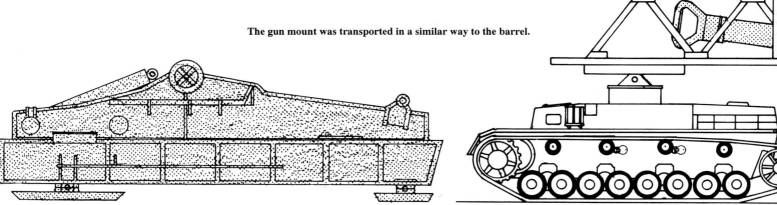

The assembly of series-production vehicles took place at the Deutsche Eisenwerke in Duisburg. Along with new chassis assembled at Nibelungenwerk, repaired chassis were also transferred regularly. The armored bodies were delivered by the Bismarckhütte firm. While the first vehicles were still fitted with the "Fahrersehklappe 80" visor of the Tiger I tank, this was eliminated in series production and replaced by a periscope. Finally, the superstructure was basically changed, with the front plate now being made of a single plate. An MG 34 was mounted in a "Kugelblende 80" ball mount above the driver. Skoda had been given a contract for 450 units of the Sturmhaubitze 43, the appearance of which also changed during the course of production. By March of 1945, 246 new vehicles of this type were built, with another 60 built on repaired chassis.

On November 4, 1944 Hitler received proposals in the form of drawings and technical data on the design of the 38 cm Wurfgeräte [launcher] on a "Hummel" chassis. Hitler considered supplying it with ammunition from a second vehicle during combat to be too difficult, and asked for a summary of experience reports on the Sturmtiger before making a decision. Hitler was convinced that the heavy armor of the Sturmtiger and carrying a sufficient supply of ammunition in the same vehicle were the basic requirements for a valuable combat vehicle.

The project of the 38 cm launcher on a Panzer IV chassis was not developed any farther.

In October of 1942 Hitler had already considered making a 30.5 cm howitzer, which was to be developed, mobile on a Panzer IV chassis as well as the 21 or 22 cm mortars. The development of these mobile howitzers, whose design was finished in 1944, could no longer be completed. The barrel, fitted with a muzzle brake, had a length of 9140 mm, and its range was planned for 24 kilometers. Emphasis was placed on simplicity of design and production as well as great mobility.

The weapon was to be transported in two loads, one for the barrel with recoil apparatus and barrel supports and the other for the carriage. It was planned that the loads would be suspended from a girder bridge attached to a Panzer III/IV chassis at each end. The carrier vehicles were designated Gerät 565, or Lastungsträger [load carrier] 604/74 for a 30.5 cm Mortar on Panzer III/IV chassis. The weight of the weapon ready to fire was some 50 tons.

Guderian wrote of it in his book: ". . . as interesting as all these designs may have been, in actual fact they all depended on the production of our only usable tank at that time, the Panzer IV, the production of which had for the first time reached the really modest number of 100 units this month . . ."

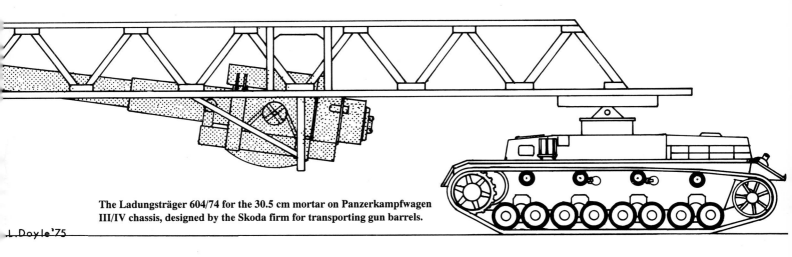

The Ladungsträger 604/74 for the 30.5 cm mortar on Panzerkampfwagen III/IV chassis, designed by the Skoda firm for transporting gun barrels.

L. Doyle '75

Flakpanzer

The problem of providing the troop units of the German Wehrmacht with protection from aircraft became more urgent and expressly required new solutions. Armored vehicles were defenseless against fighter-bombers attacking them in direct flight. In North Africa in 1942, a number of armored vehicles had been lost to low-level fighter-bomber attacks, which weakened the troops considerably.

In the further course of the war, the Allied air superiority became so oppressive that the movement of armored units became almost impossible. Generaloberst Guderian thus requested an effective defense against low-level aircraft for his Panzer units, whether in transport, while taking positions or in combat.

As was done in developing the Panzerjäger, self-propelled mounts were built at first. Available light anti-aircraft guns were mounted on tank chassis and a super-structure of armor plate was added to protect the crews.

When the gun was swung in certain directions, the walls of this superstructure had to be folded down completely or partly. The crews (up to nine men) of anti-aircraft guns many duties to perform including range-finding and aiming. These tasks could only be accomplished to a certain extent within the confines of an armored vehicle. The light anti-aircraft guns that were available were quite unsuited for being mounted on self-propelled chassis, especially as to their ammunition feed by magazines or clips, unfavorable optical and aiming equipment, and the fact that the crew could not be turned along with the gun. For these reasons, Wa Prüf 6 decided to create a new self-propelled mount design. The first vehicles of this kind were the 141 Fla-Sfl built on the 38 (t) tank chassis by the Böhmisch-Mährische Maschinenfabrik in Prague in 1943.

The meager firepower of this vehicle inspired thoughts of using the chassis of the Panzer IV as a self-propelled mount for the quadruple 2 cm Flakvierling 38 or the 3.7 cm

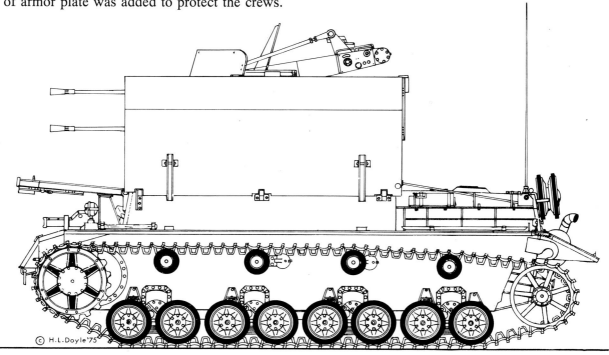

The 2 cm Flakvierling 38 auf Selbstfahrlafette Panzerkampfwagen IV

Flak 43 anti-aircraft guns. Hitler, who had still rejected this makeshift solution on May 14, 1943, requested a study in October of that year to see whether such a solution on the Panzer IV chassis would not be of more expense than it was worth, since it offered its crew protection only from shrapnel. Toward the end of 1943 the first prototype was running. It was displayed to Hitler on December 7, 1943. The vehicle

The first prototype of the self-propelled anti-aircraft gun had quadruple 2 cm Flakvierling 38 guns mounted on a Panzer IV chassis. The radio operator's machine gun had been eliminated. The upper left photograph shows the vehicle with its panels closed. Only one prototype of this vehicle was built.

For use against ground targets, the front panel was lowered. The weapons themselves were protected by a shield.

To give the crew sufficient room, it was possible to fold all the side panels down horizontally. The gun platform was expanded considerably, but no protection was afforded.

The version with the 3.7 cm Flak 43 anti-aircraft gun had the same type of superstructure as the prototype. This type was nicknamed "Möbelwagen" [moving van] because of its appearance. The photograph above shows the vehicle with its upper panels locked upright.

In action, some or all of the upper panels could be folded down.

3.7 cm Flak 43 auf Selbstfahrlafette Panzerkampfwagen IV, "Möbelwagen"

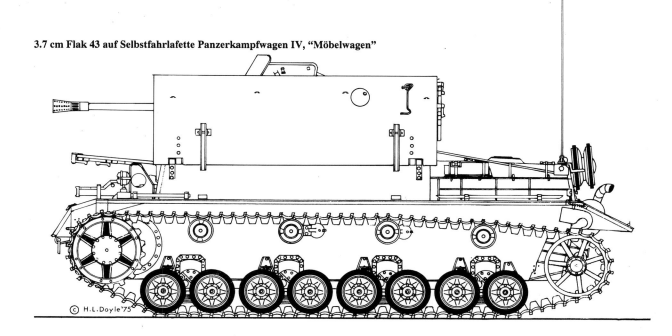

© H.L.Doyle '75

had a five-man crew and a fighting weight of 25 tons. Of the vehicle with the quadruple Flakvierling 38 guns only prototypes were built. Because of their overall height of over three meters, the troops gave it the nickname "Möbelwagen" [moving van]. The folding panels of the superstructure were 10 mm thick.

On January 28, 1944 it was decided to utilize the 3.7 cm Flak 43 gun as well. For the first time, twenty of them were to be taken from production in February and prepared as quickly as possible, and from then on, twenty of these vehicles were to be turned out every month. The 3.7 cm Panzerflak self-propelled mount on the Panzer IV chassis had a seven-man crew and an ammunition supply of 416 rounds. By partially lowering the weapon into the fighting compartment, the overall height of the vehicle was to be decreased. The superstructures with folding sides were originally delivered by the Krupp firm in Essen, and later by the Deutsche Röhrenwerke AG in Mülheim on the Ruhr. The chassis used were mainly those produced by Krupp-Gruson. In the Panzer IV chassis used with anti-aircraft guns, the engine power was somewhat increased to 272 HP by raising the engine speed from 2600 to 2800 rpm. The weapons were developed by Rheinmetall-Dürkopp-Simson

in Suhl. There were about 240 of the 3.7 cm Flakpanzer IV "Möbelwagen" built.

The crew was sometimes reduced to four men in service. While the folding armor panels of this type were originally made of two 10 mm plates fitted like bulkheads, later to facilitate production, only 20 mm sides were used.

On April 7, 1944 Hitler could be informed that the first twenty self-propelled anti-aircraft mounts with 3.7 cm Flak 43 guns on Panzer IV chassis had been prepared for delivery in March on schedule. Hitler expressed the wish that all Panzerflak self-propelled mounts built to date should be put into service in the West. In the spring of 1944, the Inspector for the Panzer Troops (In 6) took the position, that in their previous form, all self-propelled anti-aircraft mounts on halftrack and fully tracked chassis, were unsuitable for deployment in the Panzer units. He requested continued production of Flakpanzer and established the following design specifications for them:

—a rotating, fully armored turret with a 3- to 4-man crew

—effective engagement of targets within a range of 2000 meters

—at least twin guns

—a sufficient supply of ammunition

German anti-aircraft tanks on Panzer IV chassis in 1944, at left a "Möbelwagen", above the "Wirbelwind" and at right the "Ostwind" anti-aircraft tank.

At left the "Ostwind", in the center a "Möbelwagen" (3.7 cm), and at right the "Wirbelwind."

Front views of the "Wirbelwind" (left) and "Ostwind" (right). The driver's area of the "Wirbelwind" was partially strengthened.

The Flakpanzer IV, 2 cm Flakvierling 38 "Wirbelwind" carried its weapons in a turret with armor plate all around and an open top.

The Flakpanzer IV 3.7 cm "Ostwind" had a turret similar to that of the "Wirbelwind" with a 3.7 cm Flak 43 gun.

This photograph shows the "Wirbelwind" Flakpanzer in firing position. The gunner and both loaders can be seen.

These two photographs show the "Wirbelwind" (above) and "Ostwind" (below) positioned to fire on aircraft targets. At each side of the engine cover of the "Wirbelwind" there was attached a container for spare gun barrels.

—an overall height under 3 meters
—full radio equipment

The new anti-aircraft turret should provide a full view for the commander plus sufficient accessibility for the turret crew. Turret ventilation and smooth surfaces were called for.

The requirements of In 6 were to be realized in the form of a quick solution, which was became known as the "Wirbelwind."

Here the 2 cm Flakvierling 38 was mounted under sufficient armor protection on a Panzer IV chassis, and the first true Flakpanzer was thus created.

In September of 1943 Hitler had finally approved the Flakpanzer IV with the twin 3.7 cm anti-aircraft guns that had been shown to him on May 14 of that year. A further version, the "3 cm Double Flak in U-boat Turret", built by either Brünn or Rheinmetall, was to come into existence soon. The supply of turrets and guns necessary for it, though, had to be taken out of U-boat production.

In May of 1944, the ideas for anti-aircraft tanks on Panzer IV chassis developed to date were shown to Generaloberst Heinz Guderian at Kummersdorf. They included, among others, a finished prototype built by the Ostbau firm. This was the already mentioned "Wirbelwind" vehicle with quadruple 2 cm Flakvierling 38 guns. Flakzwilling 43 twin guns with over-and-under barrels, still in the form of a wooden mockup, was proposed by the ALKETT firm. The "Kugelblitz", an idea of Oberleutnant Josef von Glatter-Götz of In 6, who conceived this Flakpanzer in cooperation with Daimler-Benz, was present in drawing form. This proposed design included two 3 cm MK 103/38 guns.

Guderian decided in favor of the immediate start of series production for the "Wirbelwind", as well as the further development by Daimler-Benz in Berlin-Marienfelde of the "Kugelblitz" as a final solution.

The "Wirbelwind" design already met most of the requirements established by In 6. The rotating turret had to be redesigned. It consisted of 16 mm steel plates welded together, with a 30 mm baseplate. The originally vision ports planned in the turret for the crew could not be included for lack of time. The turret remained open at the top, but clever angled positioning of the armor plates

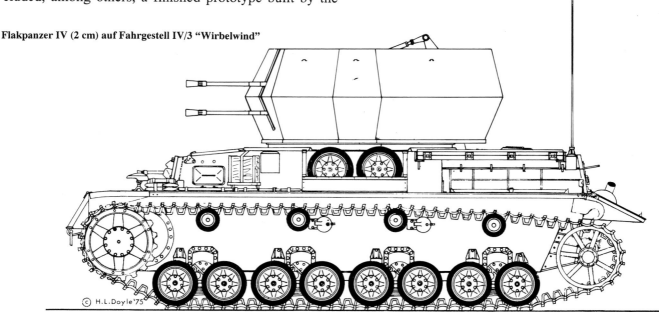

Flakpanzer IV (2 cm) auf Fahrgestell IV/3 "Wirbelwind"

decreased the remaining opening considerably from that of the self-propelled mount. Since radar was not yet in use, an unobstructed upward view had to be provided. The top of the turret had to be protected from hand grenades by an opening wire grid. A covering made of canvas provided protection against the elements. The turret was mounted on the normal Panzer IV turning ring, with a diameter of 1640 mm. Housed in the turret were the gunner, the commander beside him, and the two loaders, one on each side of the quadruple guns. By partly sinking the guns in the fighting compartment, so that the crewmen's legs extended into the hull from the knees down, the turret height could be kept at 1050 mm. Thus the overall height of the vehicle was only 2760 mm. The first test model of the turret was completed by Daimler-Benz at Marienfelde. The traversing speed of the turret was 28 degrees per second when the movement was activated mechanically by a handwheel. As an improvement, DVL installed a hydraulic traversing gear that allowed a traversing speed of 60 degrees per second. The sighting optics that were used allowed firing on air and ground targets.

The "Flakpanzer IV (2 cm) mit Fahrgestell Panzer IV/3" (Wirbelwind) had a fighting weight of 22 tons. The 90 magazine boxes could hold 3200 rounds of anti-aircraft ammunition. Containers for spare barrels were available on both sides of the engine compartment.

The anti-aircraft turrets were produced by the Deutsche Röhrenwerke AG's Thyssen Works at Mülheim on the Ruhr, but the last production turrets came from Teplitz-Schönau. The simplified quadruple Flak guns, the so-called "Sagan Geräte", were made by the Ostmark-Werke in Vienna.

The chassis for the "Wirbelwind" and later "Ostwind" vehicles were mostly taken from rebuilt and repaired Panzer IV. The assembly of the "Wirbelwind" was done by the OKH created "Ostbau" in Sagan, Silesia, under the direction of Leutnant Graf Seherr-Thoss. In all, 105 were built. About 100 of these vehicles were completed at Sagan; as of February 1945, the vehicles were built at Teplitz-Schönau. The Ostbau works at Sagan had taken on the job of preparing the turrets, which had been originally assembled by FAMO in Breslau. Along with producing small parts and delivering all of the equipment used by the troops, Ostbau also handled the complete assembly of the Flakpanzer until it was ready for the Army to accept.

At Teplitz-Schönau, the Deutsche Eisenwerke AG's Stahlindustrie works and Ostbau had set up joint production facilities, and after completely vacating the Sagan factory, Ostbau had moved the greater part of the machine tools needed for production to Teplitz. As of March 1944, a similar vehicle, also developed by Ostbau and using the new 3.7 cm Flak 43 gun, was also available. A contract for 100 of these vehicles had been given on August 18, 1944. The vehicle was ready for series production in September of 1944, but because of raw-material shortages, production could begin only in November of that year. The prototype of the "Ostwind", with a soft-steel turret made of 10 mm plates, was used in the Ardennes offensive and returned to the factory unharmed.

In the production model of the "leichte Flakpanzer mit 3.7 cm Flak 43 auf Panzerkampfwagen IV" (Ostwind), the thickness of the turret armor was increased to 25 mm. Compared to that of the "Wirbelwind", the turret was somewhat lower, measuring 1000 mm, but roomier. The 3.7 cm Flak gun had been simplified, and the lower mount had been eliminated. More than 1000 rounds of ammunition could be carried. Only one loader was now needed. Full radio equipment was now available to all the crewmen. The sliding-ring electrical contact designed for the "Panther" tank was utilized. The gun sight with elliptical plates came from the optical works of Josef Schneider & Co. in Bad Kreuznach. The elevation gear was produced by the Ostmark-Werke GmbH in Vienna. Series production, which began in November of 1944, was carried out by the Deutsche Eisenwerke AG, Werk Stahlindustrie in Duisburg at first, and then exclusively at Teplitz-Schönau.

The following schedule was established for Flakpanzer production from August through March 1945:

| | 1944 | | | | | 1945 | | |
Production Quota	Aug.	Sep.	Oct.	Nov.	Dec.	Jan.	Feb.	Mar.
Möbelwagen	30	30	20	15		runs out		
Kugelblitz	–	5	10	2	3	20	30	30
Ostwind	–	28	27	10		runs out		

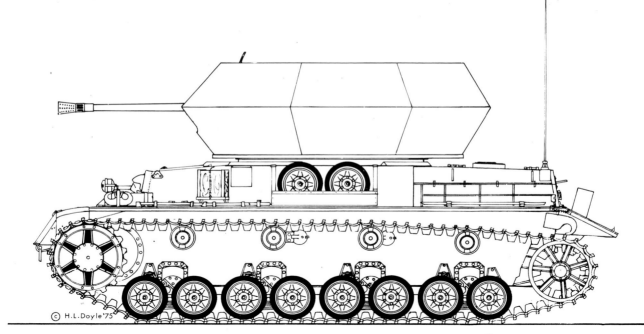

Leichter Flakpanzer mit 3.7 cm Flak 43 auf Panzerkampfwagen IV, "Ostwind"

The transition to the "Kugelblitz" was not achieved, what with starting difficulties and energy shortages. Because of delays in the start of "Ostwind" production, an additional 25 Möbelwagen were contracted. The resulting production and delivery was as follows:

	Möbelwagen (built new)	Wirbelwind (rebuilt)	Ostwind I (rebuilt)	Prototypes (rebuilt)
1944 March	20	–	–	–
April	20	–	–	–
May	15	–	–	Wirbelwind
June	34	–	–	–
July	31	–	–	Ostwind I
August	30	22	–	–
September	24	30	–	–
October	14	10	–	–
November	10	30	–	–
December	7	8	15	Zerst. 45
1945 January	5	3	13	Ostwind II
February	18	2	7	5 Kugelblitz
March	12	–	8	–
Total	240	105	43	9

Using the same type of anti-aircraft turrets, the Ostbau firm continued Flakpanzer development in the direction of higher firepower. Out of the "Wirbelwind" there arose the "Zerstörer 45" vehicle, for which quadruple 3 cm Flakvierling 103/28 guns were intended. This weapon, with a triangular mount, was first built on a "Möbelwagen" chassis for testing purposes, and was to be installed in the turret of a "Wirbelwind" later. The distance between the upper and lower barrels was greater than that of the quadruple 2 cm Flakvierling 38 guns.

The "Ostwind II" vehicle carried twin 3.7 cm Flakzwilling 44 guns in an unmodified turret. The two barrels were mounted side by side at a distance of 300 mm. Two loaders were necessary. The weapons were made by the Gustloff-Werke in Suhl. The two prototypes were built with the same external measurements as their forerunners. They had the highest firepower of any Flakpanzer used in World War II.

On April 20, 1944 Hitler ordered that since the twin 3 cm Doppelflak 303 was just going into production and the units produced in the first few months were needed exclusively to arm U-boats, the final 3 cm double-flak turret, with 60 mm armor on the Panzer IV chassis should be designed so that at first two 2 cm Flak guns could be

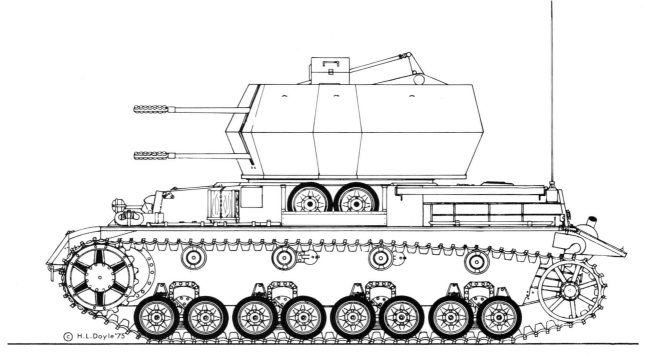

Flakpanzer (3 cm Flakvierling 103/38) "Zerstörer 45" – prototype

installed, and could be replaced later. The vehicle used for this version had to go into production as fast as possible. Series production of the 3 cm Maschinenkanone [machine cannon], though, never got started, although in mid-August 1944 Hitler was still urging the conclusion, as quickly as possible, of developmental work on the 3 cm MK 303 (Brünn) gun.

On November 4, 1944 Hitler was informed, in the form of photographs, on the further development of the Flakpanzer, with special reference to the sought-after transitional form of the "Kugelblitz" on the Panzer IV chassis.

This was the final form established for the Flakpanzer turret. Working from proposals by Oberleutnant Josef von Glatter-Götz, the Daimler-Benz AG took on the design work. The way to the "Kugelblitz" led to the 3 cm MK 103 of the Rheinmetall firm as an anti-aircraft weapon that was designated the 3 cm Flak 103/38 when it was introduced. Originally introduced as an aircraft gun, it was readily available for application as an anti-aircraft weapon. Its compact dimensions and its firepower were magnified by the fact that it was a weapon with belt feed. Its first conversion to a mechanical cocking and firing system was undertaken by the Ostbau firm. The Guben works of the Rheinmetall AG took up this version and prepared it for series production. Rheinmetall even created a special anti-aircraft barrel with a length of 2.3 meters (formerly 1.61 meters) for this weapon, which considerably improved the gun's performance. It had a cadence of 425 rounds per minute with a combat range of 5700 meters. Its two types of ammunition had a greater effect on a target than that of the 2 cm Flak gun. Ostbau immediately mounted this weapon on the 2 cm Flak field mount and gathered the first experiences with belt feed from a case of 30 to 40 rounds. This was the first belt-feed cannon in the German Army, a considerable advance over the magazines and clips used previously, but also an unqualified requirement for use within an armored vehicle. A thousand units of the 3 cm Flak 103/38 on the field mount, the so-called "Jabo-Schreck", were ordered from and delivered by the Gustloff 9-Simson) Works in Suhl, Thuringia. They were also mounted on the Steyr Type 1500 A truck, a development by the Gaubschat firm in Berlin, with Gaubschat and Ostbau each producing a series.

The Flak turret of the "Kugelblitz" with 20 mm armor consisted of a ball housing closed at the top, in which two MK 103/38 guns and a three-man crew were housed. The ball housing hung by two attachments in a truncated-wedge-shaped protective mantle. To equalize the weight at

The "Kugelblitz" Flakpanzer, finished only at the end of the war, was the first to have a fully enclosed upper body, in which two 3 cm "MK 103" guns were mounted.

The last turret of the "Kugelblitz" shows the ball housing under its protective cover and the twin guns.

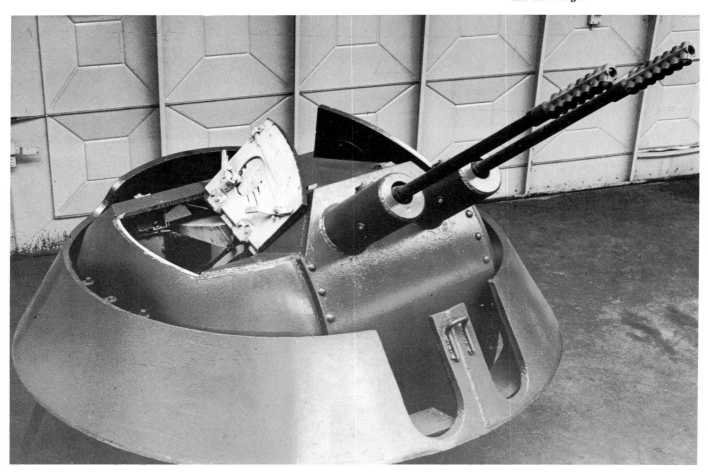

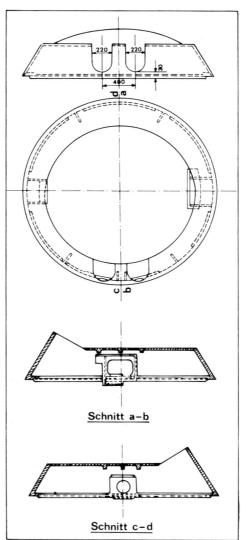

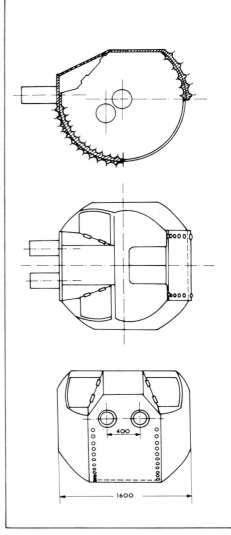

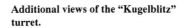

Schnitt a–b

Schnitt c–d

Additional views of the "Kugelblitz" turret.

These drawings complement the photographs.

The entry hatches for the turret crew in the ball housing.

the various degrees of elevation of the cap, an air equalizer was used. The ball housing and protective mantle were mounted on the turret race of the Tiger I tank, which had a diameter of 1900 mm. The turret had an overall height of 60 cm. This gave the vehicle an overall height of 2300 mm. The elevation range went from -7 to +80 degrees. The traversing speed was 60 degrees per second. Since hand traverse proved to be too slow, DVL installed a hydraulic drive mechanism with a control stick. A stereo-visor was completely protected by armor, and the commander advised the gunner of the target by using an indicator device. In the final turret, the commander was supposed to sit under a small cupola. He observed with periscope and angled telescope, the latter of which could be used simultaneously as a stereoscopic range finder. The two guns were mounted in the turret and equipped with an exhaust blower for the propellant fumes. The ammunition was fed in belts through sheet-metal chutes. The total supply was 1200 rounds of 3 cm ammunition. Cases and belt links were deposited in a linen bag directly under the weapons.

Although the Heeresverordnungsblatt 1944 No. 761 proclaimed the introduction of this vehicle, only a pre-series of five vehicles was built. It carried the official designation "leichte Flakpanzer IV (3 cm)" (Kugelblitz). It was supposed to replace the "leichte Flakpanzer mit 3.7 cm Flak 43 auf Panzer IV" (Möbelwagen) in January of 1945 and go into series production in February 1945, at a rate of 30 units per month.

The pre-series of the "Kugelblitz" were to be assembled by Daimler-Benz and delivered in March/April 1945. The vehicles were to be issued to the Panzer-Flak replacement and training unit. A special unit was to be created consisting of platoons with six "Wirbelwind", "Kugelblitz", "Ostwind" or "Möbelwagen" Flakpanzer. In 1944, Flakpanzer platoons were formed and assigned to Panzer-Regiments and Abteilungen. These normally were issued eight of the "Möbelwagen" or four "Möbelwagen" and four "Wirbelwind" Flakpanzer.

It is interesting to note that in November of 1944 Hitler accepted, as the final product of Flakpanzer development, the use of the "Kugelblitz" turret with two rapid-fire cannons (originally MK 103) on the chassis of the "Hetzer" Panzerjäger. It was planned to have an MG 151/20 machine gun on each side of the two 3 cm cannons. Hitler considered this solution to be especially noteworthy and ordered production started as soon as possible, including both the final type and the transitional type on the Panzer IV chassis. As also happened with other wishes of the troops, Flakpanzer development suffered in 1944 from the typical problems of the year. Yet its modern conception still served as a guide until the end of the fifties.

Leichter Flakpanzer IV (3 cm) "Kugelblitz"

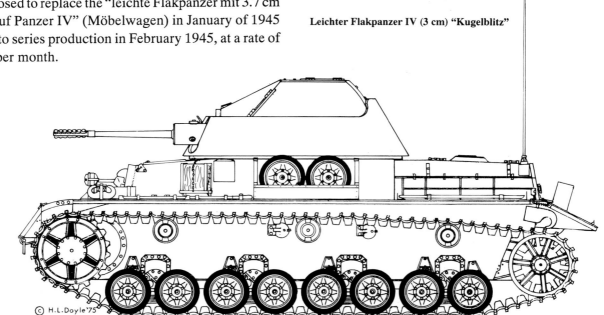

Self-Propelled Mounts

The experiences gained in the campaigns of World War II soon resulted, in the motorized artillery and particularly in the armored artillery, in a series of tactical requirements that now drew clear dividing lines against the already obsolete concepts of self-propelled artillery mounts. As opposed to the tanks that were to be supported, it proved to be necessary to require higher driving performance to be able to guarantee the "keeping up" and "swinging along" of the artillery in a progressive tank attack. The distance between the tanks and the artillery, which was steadily growing larger, had to be covered in the shortest possible time when positions were changed, so as to guarantee artillery support at any time.

In addition the ability to quickly engage targets was necessary, since the armored artillery was constantly on its own in areas that were traversed only by tanks. Reviving enemy resistance had to be eliminated quickly and effectively. This required all-around fire. This requirement for all-around fire was not at all met by turning the entire vehicle. These turning movements were too slow and imprecise in artillery terms.

Since the armored artillery, and therefore the self-propelled artillery, were indispensable in defensive actions, and on the other hand the valuable vehicles should not be exposed unnecessarily to enemy fire and weather, dismounting the gun became a requirement. The value of the self-propelled mount was its high degree of mobility, which required constant maintenance. In a firing position this was only possible within certain limits. In addition, a dismounted gun provided a considerably smaller target in defensive action.

Then too, the self-propelled artillery had to in any case remain artillery, and could not be employed as a Sturmgeschütz or Panzerkampfwagen, since it would then no longer be able to fulfill its artillery tasks. Armor protection needed to be sufficient to stop the penetration by armor piercing projectiles fired by small arms and shell fragments. The weight savings by the thinner armor plates could benefit its mobility.

The ammunition unit of a self-propelled gun battery should, for practical purposes, be equipped with the same type of tracked vehicles. If a gun carriage was put out of action, the possibility of transferring the gun to an ammunition carrier should exist.

While a final solution to this requirement was being worked on since the beginning of 1942, there were transitional solutions caused by the urgency of equipping the armored artillery, achieved by utilizing already existing components. For the purpose of saving time, as many components as possible that were already in production were used. A field of elevation from -8 to +40 degrees and a field of traverse extending 35 degrees to each side were prescribed.

For the schwere Feldhaubitze 18 [heavy field howitzer], the use of a Panzer III/IV chassis was planned. In order to create a roomy fighting compartment, the engine was moved to the middle. The manufacture of the components linking the gun and the vehicle had to be done quickly and simply, since the production of certain quantities of equipment in a short time was required. Machine work and the use of adapters had to be limited to what was absolutely necessary.

The Alkett in Borsigwalde began this development in 1942 and created the "Geschützwagen III/IV" gun carriage. The contract called for the creation of a makeshift solution in a very short developmental time, with the use of available gun and vehicle components for the heavy howitzer. For the sFH 18 howitzer, components of the Panzer III or IV were thus put to use to form a chassis. The following list shows the origins of the components used in the Geschützwagen III/IV:

Group	Components	Origin	Notes
Running gear	Road wheels	Panzer IV Ausf. F	
	Wheel mounts	Panzer IV Ausf. F	
	Return rollers	Panzer IV Ausf. F	
	Suspension	Panzer IV Ausf. F	
	Buffer stops	Panzer IV Ausf. F	
	Leading wheels	Panzer IV Ausf. F	
	Tracks	Panzer IV Ausf. F	400 mm wide
	Track tensioner	Panzer IV Ausf. F	
Drive	Drive wheels	Panzer III Ausf. J	
	Final drives	Panzer III Ausf. J	
	Brakes	Panzer III Ausf. J	mechanical
	SSG 77 transmission	Panzer III Ausf. J	
	Driveshaft	pecially made	165 mm long
Engine	Maybach HL 120 TRM	Panzer III	minus exhaust fittings etc.
	Exhaust pipe	Specially made	
	Oil filler	Specially made	
	Fuel pump	Panzer III	Panzer IV can be adapted
	Electric fuel pump	Panzer III	
	Fuel filter	Panzer III	
	Air filter	Panzer IV	
	Radiator	Panzer IV	
	Cooling fans	Panzer IV	
	Fan drive tensioner	Panzer IV	
	Fan drive belt	Panzer III	
	Fan drives	Specially made	fits Panzer IV
	Muffler	Panzer IV	
	Batteries	Panzer III	two 12-volt

The inertia starter, fuel lines, central lubrication, and winter equipment were special parts.

Under the existing conditions it was not possible to enable all-around fire and removal of the gun by expedient measures. The high power-to-weight ratio required for self-propelled artillery mounts could not be attained either, as existing powerplants had to be utilized. But the communications equipment of the transitional type was made so that the organizational experience could already be utilized for the final version. This was all the more important because the armored artillery observation vehicle (Panzer III transitional type) likewise was equipped with the final version of the communications equipment.

In July of 1942 it was reported that after the light field howitzer could be mounted on the Panzer II chassis, the planned Panzer III/IV chassis was to be produced quickly and used to build 200 self-propelled mounts for heavy field howitzers. They were to be finished by May 12, 1943. ALKETT had originally envisioned the following uses for the Panzer III/IV chassis:

Gerät 804 Geschützwagen III/IV für leFH 18/40/2 Sf,
Gerät 807 Geschützwagen III/IV für sFH 18/1 Sf, and
Gerät 812 Geschützwagen III/IV für sFH 18/5 Sf.

In October of 1942 Hitler was shown a soft steel model of the self-propelled mount for the 8.8 cm Pak 43/1 L/71 and the 15 cm sFH 81/1 guns, which used the same components. Hitler expressed his satisfaction and looked forward to the arrival of the expected production of 100 units each by May 12, 1943.

Although Hitler regarded the lightly armored self-propelled mount for the 8.8 cm Pak as only an expedient or transitional measure in February of 1943, the 100 units were to be produced by May 12. Beginning in May, the production rate was to be reduced to 20 units per month in order to produce the self-propelled howitzer at a higher rate.

The series production of the "8.8 cm Pak 43/1 (L/71) auf Fahrgestell Panzerkampfwagen III/IV (Sf) (Sd.Kfz.164)" began at the Deutsche Eisenwerke in Teplitz-Schönau. The chassis number series began with 310001, and the chassis were provided by the Duisburg factory of the same firm. The armor came from the Witkowitzer Bergbau und Eisenhütten Gewerkschaft. The name of "Hornisse" (Hornet) was replaced by "Nashorn" (Rhinoceros) by the Führer's order on January 27, 1944. In all, 494 units were produced by 1945.

The mounting of the sFH 18/1 armo ·d howitzer on the Panzerkampfwagen III/IV (Sf) (Sd.Kfz.165) took place at

8.8 cm Pak 43/1 (L/71) auf
Fahrgestell III/IV (Sf)
(Sd.Kfz.164) "Nashorn",
formerly "Hornisse."

© H.L.Doyle '75

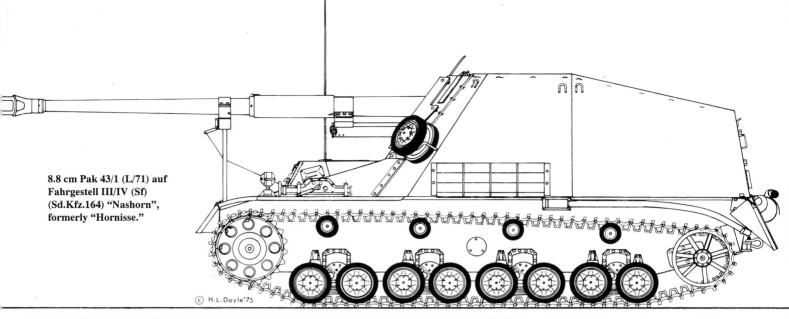

One of the first self-propelled 8.8 cm Pak 43/1 guns on Gw III/IV chassis. The vehicle still has the old Panzer III drive wheels, with a device attached for measuring vertical movements. These vehicles could not be put into service until a practical travel lock for the gun barrel was developed.

The production model
"8.8 cm Pak 43/1 (L.71)
auf Fahrgestell III/IV (Sf)
– Nashorn, formerly
Hornisse (Sd.Kfz.164)."

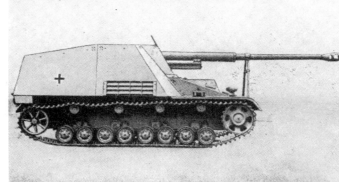

Front and side views of the "Hornisse", Sd.Kfz.164.

The "Hornisse" in service in Russia. The upper right photograph shows a rear view with opened rear hatch to the open-topped fighting compartment.

These two photographs show the "Hornisse" (above) and "Hummel" (below).

These two photographs show a "Hummel" of the Waffen-SS, notable for several reasons. The top of the fighting compartment is covered by a folding grid screen, and the vehicle bears a registration number.

For comparison, here is an Army vehicle that is just being prepared to fire.

A view of the fighting compartment toward the breech of the 15 cm howitzer.

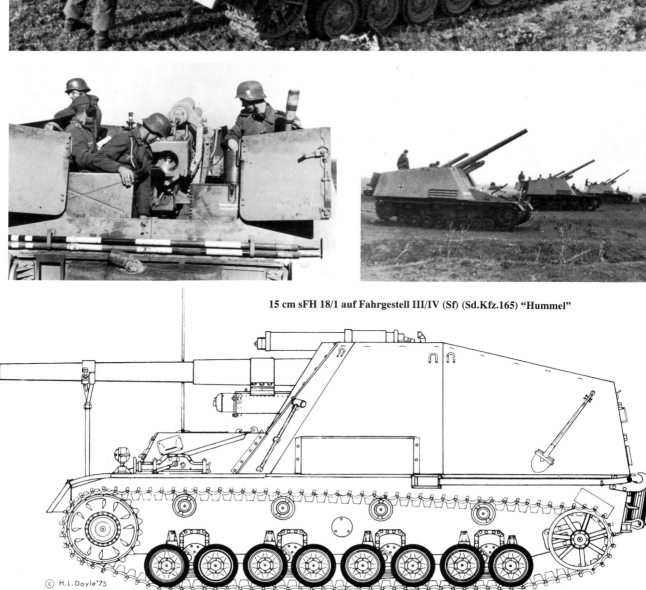

15 cm sFH 18/1 auf Fahrgestell III/IV (Sf) (Sd.Kfz.165) "Hummel"

© H.L.Doyle '75

Upper left: A Munitionsträger crosses a river. It was built exactly like the Geschützwagen III/IV but had no armament. It was used to supply the howitzer batteries with ammunition.

Left center: The final design of the driver's compartment of the "Hummel" (Sd.Kfz.165).

Upper right: The folding travel lock was attached to the glacis plate.

Right center: Most of the first 500 vehicles built had the narrower driver's compartment, which made observation to the sides much easier.

Munitionsträger auf Fahrgestell III/IV

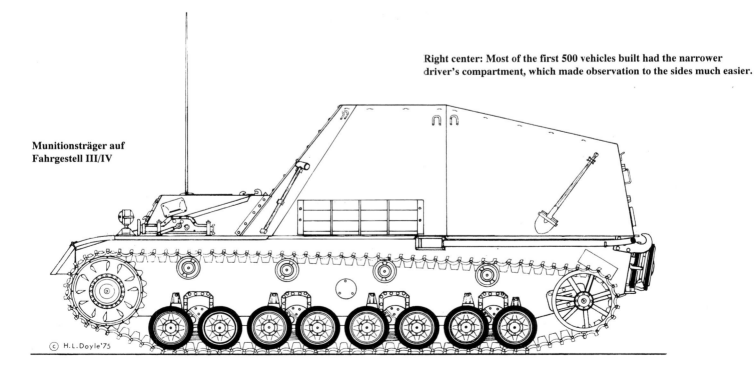

© H.L.Doyle '75

the Deutsche Eisenwerke in Duisburg. The armor plate was produced by the Deutsche Röhrenwerke in Mülheim. The chassis number series began with 320001. While the ALKETT prototypes still had a muzzle brake, this was completely eliminated according to Army Technical Instruction No. 411 of 1944. The use of the 8th charge was then forbidden. There were 724 units (ten via rebuilding) of this vehicle built under the name of "Hummel" (Bumblebee), as well as 157 "Munitionsträger" [ammunition carriers]. The name of "Hummel" was eliminated by the Führer's order on February 27, 1944.

The construction of the driver's compartment of these vehicles underwent changes during the course of its development.

In May of 1943 it was reported to Hitler that, because of the temporary shortage of engines and gearboxes at that time, the planned production quotas for the "Hummel" and "Hornisse" could not be met fully. According to Hitler's instructions, it was of primary importance that engines and gearboxes were to be built first in sufficient numbers for all available tank hulls. But since these two vehicles were likewise urgent, Hitler expected that manufacturing at new capacity levels would assuredly begin as soon as possible. In addition, Hitler considered the determination of building capacities for the Geschützwagen III/IV not to be appropriate until the first reports of front-line experience had arrived. On June 28, 1943 Speer had to report that the completed "Hornisse" vehicles were not ready for action, for the vehicles could not be driven due to an inadequate travel lock for the gun. Since the troops were already equipped with them beginning in May of 1943, the elimination of this fault was urgent. By the end of June 1943 there were already 85 "Hornisse" units in service at the front. The "Hummel" vehicle likewise reached the front in May of 1943. By December 227 units had been delivered. In all, 368 of them were built in 1943.

In August of 1943 the possibility of using the chassis of the Geschützwagen III/IV as a carrier for the light howitzer on a special mount with the barrel of the leFH 43 howitzer. The possibility of lifting it off the carrier was to be investigated as before. This could result in the final form of a self-propelled mount for the light howitzer, even though under the given requirements the demand for all-around fire would have to be given up. A decision made on September 11, 1943, though, still foresaw the following developments:

–leFH 18/40 with all-around fire on Zgkw. 3t, dismountable, on a cruciform mount,

–Pak 44 (7.5 cm L/70) with all-around fire on Zgkw. 3t, dismountable, on a cruciform mount, and

–leFH 18/40 with all-around fire on Gw III/IV, dismountable, on a cruciform mount.

In fact, the establishment of a production series of self-propelled artillery ended with the Geschützwagen II and III/IV.

Now let us look more closely at the planned "final designs" for such self-propelled carriages:

The requirements for artillery and self-propelled mounts established in 1942 basically featured the following details:

–Higher driving performance compared to the tank,
–Ability to quickly engage targets,
–All-around fire,
–A dismountable gun, and
–Protection for the crew from machine-gun fire and shrapnel.

As for the development of artillery on self-propelled mounts, Hitler wanted to think over the final form of his stipulations again in April of 1942. He was basically in agreement with the proposed program, but insisted that a mobile 21 cm mortar be produced as well.

Since the self-propelled mount for the light field howitzer was a brand new design used for the first time, it was decided in July of 1942 to develop the three proposed models to the point of a first test model. In addition, the installation of the 8.8 cm Pak 43 gun with its own mount, proposed by Rheinmetall and Krupp, on the chassis of the self-propelled light howitzer mount was to be carried out as a test model.

Travel condition

Preparation to dismount

Dismounting

Turret set on the ground

Turret ready to fire

Vehicle as ammunition carrier

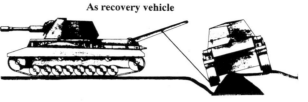

Gun on trailer

As recovery vehicle

As seen from behind

The principle of the "Heuschrecke" design for the armored artillery

The "Heuschrecke 10" vehicle towing a gun trailer.

The turret is positioned on the ground. Note that not only the lifting tackle but the pieces of the mount were carried on the vehicle.

Below: The gun turret mounted on the vehicle, capable of all-around fire.

The three available models for the self-propelled light howitzer mount had not been planned only for use with the leFH 43, but also as carriers of the 12.8 cm cannon. This development was also to be continued to the point of producing an initial test model.

Efforts were made to continue the development of self-propelled artillery mounts and weapons carriers from 1942 on independently of tank production. Krupp, Rheinmetall and Ardelt were to be the developmental firms.

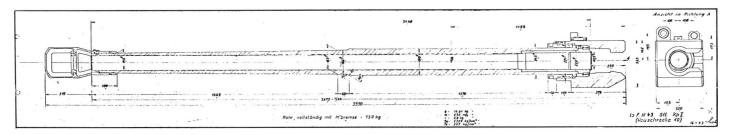

A longitudinal drawing of the gun developed by Krupp especially for this purpose, the 10.5 cm leFH 43 Sfl Kp I.

The "Heuschrecke 10" ready to march.

The Rheinmetall firm used an unmodified light field howitzer in its version, equipped it with an armored housing, and mounted it in a position on the vehicle where it could be traversed.

Photographs on the right page show side and rear views of the Rheinmetall design. The wheels for the gun carriage were carried on the rear of the vehicle.

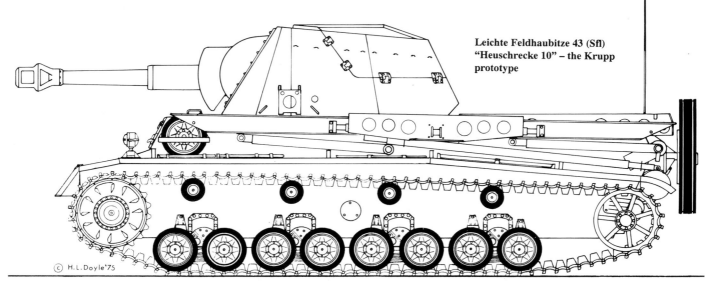

Leichte Feldhaubitze 43 (Sfl) "Heuschrecke 10" – the Krupp prototype

© H.L.Doyle'75

Components of the "Leopard" vehicle had originally been supposed to be used for the development of the self-propelled light howitzer mount. On account of the unavailability of this vehicle, components of the new assault gun (some 35 tons) were now to be used. The necessary drawings of this ALKETT design were supposed to be available no later than May 1, 1943. But so as to have test vehicles ready as soon as possible, components of the Panzer IV were used for this vehicle, with the expectation that the HL 90 (350 HP) engine would be used for the test model and the HL 100 (400 HP) engine for the final version. The prompt start of series production of these powerplants, which had

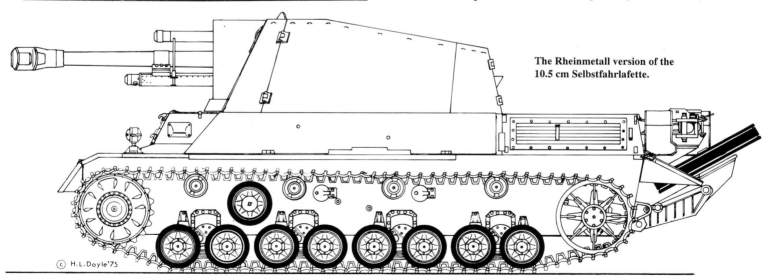

The Rheinmetall version of the 10.5 cm Selbstfahrlafette.

© H. L. Doyle '75

not been available previously, was therefore of decisive importance for the self-propelled light howitzer mount.

In the period from January 27 to 30, 1943, all the previously produced self-propelled artillery mounts were displayed in Berlin. Thus a comparative evaluation of the state of development could be undertaken according to military, technical and manufacturing standpoints. The light self-propelled mount models for the 10.5 cm leFH 43 built by Krupp, Rheinmetall-Daimler-Benz and Skoda were displayed. In terms of their design and workmanship as applied to the concept of the self-propelled mount, the Krupp "Heuschrecke" and Rheinmetall versions stood out. Krupp had deliberately disregarded the requirement to adopt components of the existing field guns as much as possible. The higher-performance barrel with a jacket cradle, built especially for the self-propelled mount and installed in a turning turret, gave the vehicle a harmoniously closed appearance but gave rise to concern in view of the production difficulties. The barrel had a length of 3675 mm (= L/35), and weighed 730 kg with a muzzle brake. The muzzle velocity was 665 meters per second.

Rheinmetall, on the other hand, utilized the field gun almost unchanged, equipped with an armored housing and carried in a traversable mount on the chassis.

Both firms solved the problem of removing the gun with the help of swinging arms, with the power coming through a geared drive in the Krupp version and hydraulically in the Rheinmetall model. Krupp set the gun on a frame that was carried on the vehicle in four sections; Rheinmetall used spars in the form of a cruciform mount. The ammunition storage (60 rounds) had been provided for very well in the Krupp version, but in the Rheinmetall model it had not yet been developed fully.

In view of the very different paths that had been followed by the two firms, a final evaluation and decision could be expected only when the results of firing, driving and gun-removing tests were at hand. Each firm was instructed to build a test model.

In addition to the "Heuschrecke", Krupp introduced another new design, though only in the form of drawings. It was based on the possibility of carrying a two-axle field gun, in a cross mount similar to that of an anti-aircraft gun, on a self-propelled mount unchanged. This suggestion was greeted with great interest, and Krupp was advised to keep a suitable self-propelled mount in mind along with the development of this two-axle field mount.

One of the Krupp prototypes of the "Heuschrecke" bore chassis number 582503. Its chassis had originally been lengthened somewhat to the rear, and the number of track links had risen from 99 to 107.

In April of 1944 Hitler had been shown pictures and technical data of both of the vehicles under development. His inclination was that despite the various disadvantages, a design had to be chosen under any conditions in which the earlier light field howitzer was used, and used, moreover, removed and set on wheels. In this way the gun would still be ready for action if the chassis were put out of action.

These two designs formed the conclusion of the development of a self-propelled light howitzer mount that had been going on since 1942.

The Krupp firm's development bore the catchall name of "Grille" (Cricket), while Rheinmetall-Borsig used the name "Skorpion."

Divided into size classes, the Type 10 was capable of carrying either the 10.5 cm leFH 43 or the 10 cm Kanone. The Type 15 could carry the 15 cm sFH 43 or the 12.8 cm Kanone 43. In addition, a Type 17/21 was also envisioned.

In the meantime, the Krupp firm had laid out the "O-Series" of a armored self-propelled mount with a chassis based on Panzer IV running gear. There were only three pairs of road wheels installed on each side. This vehicle went by the designation of "leFH 18/1 (Sf)/Gw IV b (Sd.Kfz.165/1)" and was equipped with the Maybach HL 66 engine, which was to be replaced in the production model by the 320-horsepower HL 90. The 17-ton vehicle carried the light field howitzer with a traverse field of 70 degrees in all. Elevations from -10 to +40 degrees were attainable. The barrel length of this howitzer was 2941 mm (= L.28), and the complete barrel with muzzle brake weighed 726 kg. Its muzzle velocity was 480 meters per second. Sixty rounds of ready ammunition were carried. The armor, open on top and made of 20 mm plates in front and 14.5 mm on the sides, protected a five-man crew. In November of 1942 Hitler agreed that only eight vehicles were to be

Eight of these "leFH 18/1 (Sf)/Gw IV b" (Sd.Kfz.165/1) were actually completed. Krupp utilized a shortened Panzer IV chassis with only three pairs of roadwheels per side. The photographs above show the vehicles from the left and right sides.

The rear view at the lower left shows the position of the engine compartment, the exhaust system and the track-tension device retained from the Panzer IV.

The fighting compartment, open at the top, can be seen clearly in this photograph. The sidewalls of the upper body curved outward at the sides around the turret ring.

Leichte Feldhaubitze 18/1 (Sf)/Gw IV b (Sd.Kfz.165/1)

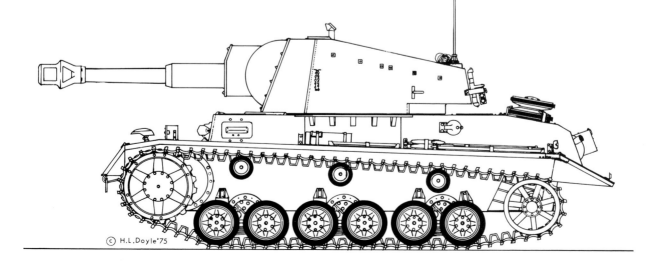

© H.L. Doyle '75

prepared to carry the leFH 18/1 on Gw IV b, which was just going into production. The complete package did not correspond to the established requirements. Later proposals were made to rebuild this self-propelled mount into a Panzerjäger vehicle (Panzerjäger IV b (E 39)).

On November 28, 1944 Speer reported, on the basis of drawings, on a "Hummel-Wespe" vehicle as a universal self-propelled artillery mount.

Hitler regarded this makeshift solution as extremely valuable. Further details of this project are no longer known.

Weapons Carriers

In the process of separating self-propelled artillery mount production from tank manufacture, the development of so-called "Waffenträger" [weapons-carriers] had been going on since 1942. The Waffenamt (Wa Prüf 4) brought firms that were not directly involved in tank production into the process.

The originally established military requirements called for, among other things:

–A fully-tracked chassis, independent of tank production, with a production engine that allowed a marching speed of about 17 km/hr.

–Provisions for dismounting the gun by means available to the troops. All equipment had to be carried on the vehicle.

–All-around fire with 360-degree traverse, both on the vehicle and when removed.

–The gun was to be mobile on its own wheeled mount.

–Shrapnel protection for the crew, 8 mm armor plate being considered sufficient.

–Uniform chassis on which a choice of several weapons could be carried.

On this basis, several developmental studies were worked out, including, among others, consideration of using chassis components of the Panzer IV and III/IV.

Wa Prüf 4 had established the following designations for these vehicles: "Einheits-Waffenträger, Grösse I" and "Einheits-Waffenträger, Grösse II" [universal weapons carries, size I and II].

Suggestions were made, involving Panzer IV or III/IV chassis components, for a "Mittleren Waffenträger [medium weapons carrier] für 15 cm sFH 18 (L/29.5)" and a "Mittleren Waffenträger für 12.8 cm K 81 (L/55)."

The first prototypes, presented by Krupp, Steyr and Rheinmetall, found only limited approval, since they had turned out to be too complicated and too ponderous. The

The Panzer IV chassis was also used in "Waffenträger" development. This drawing shows the design of a "Mittlerer Waffenträger für die 15 cm sFH 18 (L/29.5)."

The second design utilizing components of the Panzer IV chassis resulted in the "Mittlerer Waffenträger für die 12.8 cm Kanone 81 (L/55)." This design never advanced beyond the drawing board.

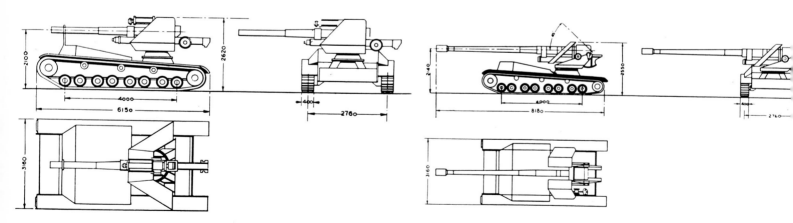

industry thereupon suggested means of simplification, and Wa Prüf 4 stated its readiness to drop some of its requirements. Despite all of this, no satisfactory solution could be found.

On February 4, 1944, on the occasion of a conference at Steyr-Daimler-Puch, a representative of Wa Prüf 4 presented requirements for a Waffenträger which had been changed again. Among other things, it was stated in them that the development of these vehicles was not to amount to a stopgap measure, meaning the placing of a weapon on an already existing chassis. The complete vehicle was to be developed especially for this purpose.

The Panzer IV and III/IV chassis were now dropped as the basis of this development, since a lighter vehicle was preferred. It should be kept in mind that at this point the Panzer IV was already regarded as a model that would not be produced indefinitely, and that it was only a matter of time until its production would be halted.

Other Types

Of the other special armored vehicles on the Panzer IV chassis, those intended for use by the armored engineer battalions as "Brückenleger" [bridgelayers] and "Infanterie-Sturmsteg" [infantry assault bridges] are particularly noteworthy. The Commander of the Army asked the Waffenamt on October 19, 1939 to take action on the manufacture of the bridgelayer vehicle, and fifty units were contracted for.

The first tests of bridgelaying tanks took place in 1939. This photograph shows two test vehicles, in the foreground a Panzer IV test chassis with an assault bridge. Both types were able to bridge both natural and man-made obstacles.

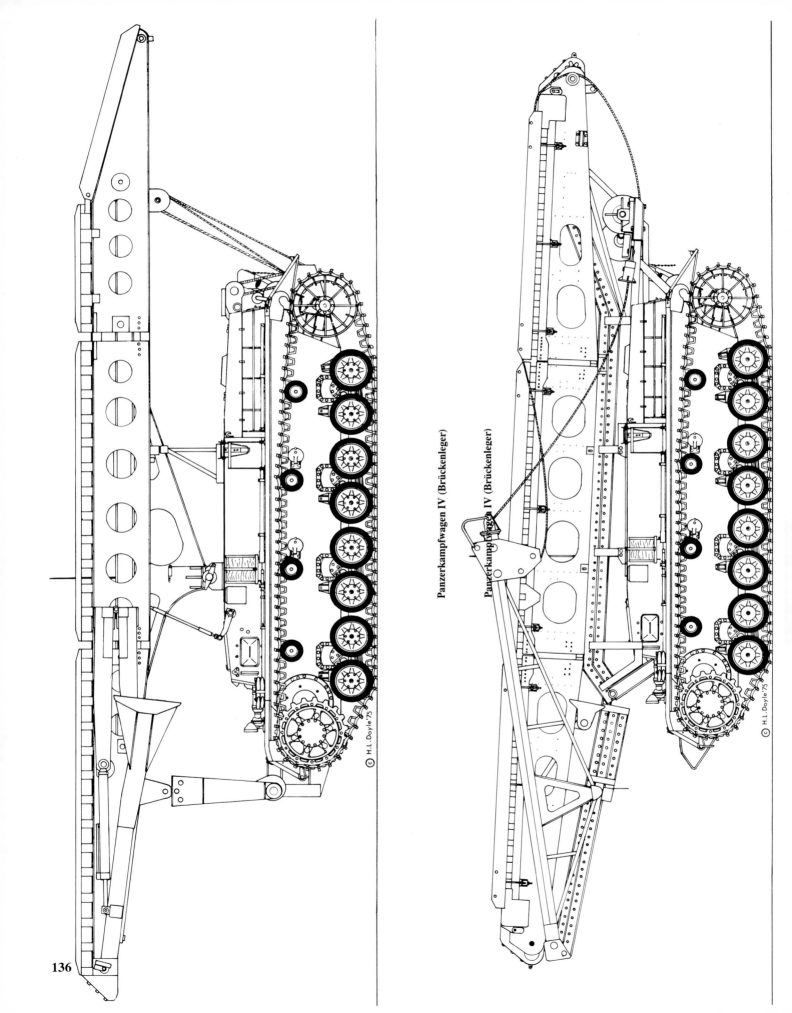

Panzerkampfwagen IV (Brückenleger)

Panzerkampfwagen IV (Brückenleger)

© H.L.Doyle '75

© H.L.Doyle '75

These photographs show the process of positioning the assault bridge. The first vehicle unloads the structure and departs.

This photograph shows the extending and positioning of the second vehicle's bridge section.

The second vehicle utilizes the first part of the bridge and prepares to unload the second part.

With the deploying of the second part of the bridge, the opening at hand is bridged and the way over the obstacle is open. This was a forward-looking approach that was also tested by the Bundeswehr.

The Panzerkampfwagen IV (Brückenleger) at upper left was mounted on a "0-Series" prototype chassis made by Krupp. The road wheels, suspended on torsion bars, were dampened by shock absorbers. Only three return rollers were used.

Six Panzer IV chassis of the Panzer IV assembled in 1939 had already been reserved for this purpose. These were Ausf. C chassis. On January 1, 1940 the Commander of the Army determined that 12 bridgelaying vehicles on Panzer IV chassis with a length of 9 meters were to be expected by the end of March, two of them coming from Krupp and the rest from Magirus. Three of these vehicles were planned for every Panzer division. Production was delayed, though, and test vehicles were delivered for Wa Prüf 4 and 5 only in February of 1940, followed by sixteen more Panzer IV chassis by April 1940. On March 2, 1940 the first assignment of these vehicles to the 1. Panzer Division took place. On March 6, 1940 it was reported that the first twenty vehicles would be ready, with trained personnel, by the end of April. Another thirty vehicles were under contract. The 1. to 5. Panzer Divisions, which at that time already included armored engineer battalions with three companies each, were to receive these vehicles. The training of the crews was to be assured by a training course created by the BdE. For the 6. to 10. Panzer Divisions, a similar training course still had to be organized. On April 19, 1940 the exhibition of a bridgelaying tank took place in Klausdorf.

The document Stab Ia No. 1016 of May 31, 1940 gave the following official information on further development. According to it, there were available:

a. One test vehicle made of soft steel, which was not suitable for combat,

b. 20 bridgelaying vehicles, in service with four bridgelayers per platoon of an engineer company, in the 1st, 2nd, 3rd, 5th and 10th Panzer Divisions,

Another sixty of these vehicles were under contract, and included

a. 12 units in improved form (to be delivered in August and September of 1940), and

b. 48 units to follow at the rate of four vehicles per month.

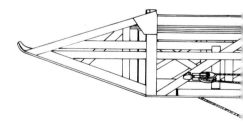

Krupp also mounted this quickly deployed bridge on a Panzerkampfwagen IV (Ausf. D) chassis. The photographs at left show two of these vehicles in action in France in 1940.

Just a month later, the situation had changed essentially. Document No. 1023.40 GKdos, of June 3, 1940, stated that the planned bridgelayers were to be dispensed with. The vehicles provided for them were to be used to increase the production of Panzer IV tanks. Two chassis that had been used for "Brückenleger" were converted back and assembled as Panzer IV in August of 1940. A decision as to a transition to the Panzer III chassis for a bridgelayer had not yet been made at this point in time. On September 24, 1940 it was reported about the bridgelayers that the bridge was now to be carried on a special vehicle. With a span of ten meters, the height of the mount was three meters. The model was to be ready for display by mid-October of 1940, and by the spring of 1941 every Panzer

To help the infantry overcome obstacles, an "Infanterie-Sturmsteg" was created, likewise mounted on a Panzer IV chassis. A mechanism similar to that of Magirus extending fire ladders was utilized. This photograph shows a model of this vehicle.

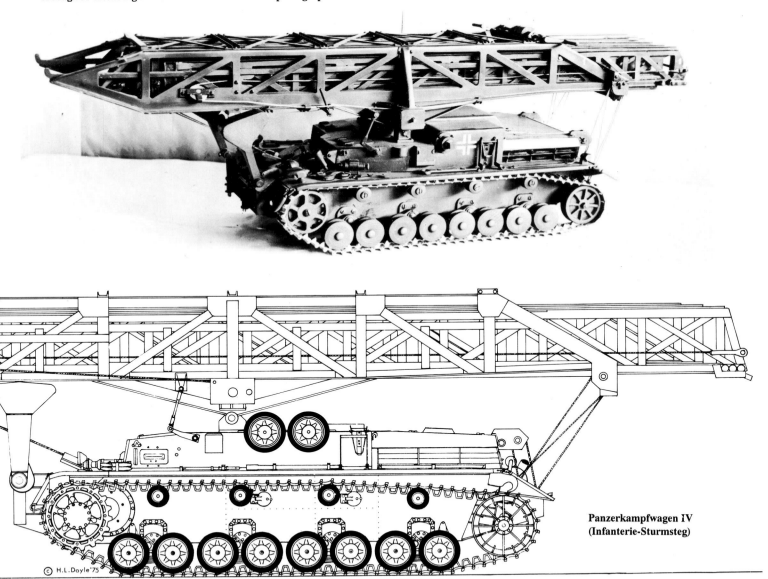

Panzerkampfwagen IV (Infanterie-Sturmsteg)

© H.L. Doyle '75

Above: The same model with its bridge extended. The vehicle had to be supported by a hydraulic jack at the front.

After two of these vehicles had extended their assault bridges, planks could be laid in the middle, making the bridge capable of carrying even small vehicles.

Several of these vehicles were actually built and utilized in Russia.

To supply ammunition to the very heavy "Gerät 040", Panzer IV chassis were fitted with modified superstructures. At the right front of this vehicle a three-ton crane was mounted to move the 2.2-ton shells. This photograph shows the "Munitionsträger für Karlgerät" from the left side.

division was to have five of them, meaning that a total of 100 units was required. On February 18, 1941 this bridge appeared in its new form, with a carrying capacity of 28 tons. Now the upper structure, divided into three loads, was loaded onto trucks. Four units were finished and sent to the 3rd Panzer Division. Here too, no usable solution was created, for Army Communique No. 117 of 1941 stated that the proposed bridgelaying platoons of the engineer companies were to be eliminated because appropriate vehicles were not available and could not be created in a short time.

The development conducted by the firm of Klöckner-Humboldt-Deutz was in the hands of Oberingenieur Dr. Oskar Herterich. Magirus was using an unchanged Panzer IV chassis. Krupp, on the other hand, was using a test chassis for its version, with six medium-sized road wheels mounted on torsion bars on each side of the vehicle.

The "Infanterie-Sturmsteg" used extending traversable ladders on the principle of the aerial-ladder fire trucks built by C. D. Magirus. Two vehicles side by side were to extend their ladders over the obstacle to be surmounted, and planks were placed between the extended ladders to create a pathway to be driven on.

Delivery of chassis for these "Infanterie-Sturmsteg" to Wa Prüf 5 took place in 1940. They were tested in Russia.

After the establishment of the heaviest artillery units (siege artillery) with the Gerät 040 (Karlgerät), of which Rheinmetall built a seven combat vehicles, a special version of the Panzer IV was introduced in that unit as an ammunition carrier. The Krupp-Gruson AG in Magdeburg delivered chassis for a number of these vehicles in 1941.

They went by the designation of "Munitionsträger für Karlgerät." These vehicles, fitted with special superstruc-

Right column, top to bottom: The ammunition carrier beside the "Gerät 040", loading it with ammunition.

Here the Munitionsträger stands beside the gun, and the shell is just being lifted off the vehicle.

Here one of the shells is being lifted out of its retainers on the ammunition carrier.

Then the shell is moved to the gun. The second shell is attached to the vehicle.

Below: A side view of the vehicle with the crane fully elevated.

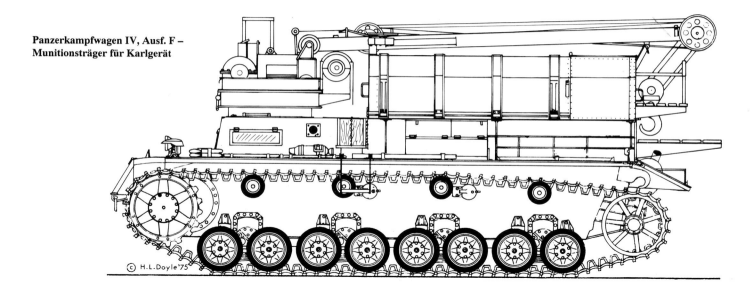

**Panzerkampfwagen IV, Ausf. F –
Munitionsträger für Karlgerät**

tures, could each carry two of the 2.2-ton 60 cm shells and load them directly onto the self-propelled mount by means of a 2.5-ton crane.

In 1936 the Army High Command contracted for a vehicle that was to serve as a towing tractor on land, a motorized towboat in the water, a tractor in shallow water and a motorized tugboat for landing craft. Wa Prüf 5 was responsible for this development and, in cooperation with several firms, created this so-called "Landwasserschlepper" [land-water tractor], an amphibious full-track vehicle of which 21 examples in all were built.

At the same time, the Kässbohrer firm in Ulm had been given a contract to develop an amphibious trailer for this vehicle.

The successor of the "Landwasserschlepper" with trailer was a so-called "Panzerfähre" (Pz.F) [armored ferry] created in 1941 at the order of the Heeres Waffenamt. On April 19, 1941 the development of a ferry-like device began; it was intended to ferry tanks up to the size of the Panzer IV and off-road wheeled vehicles. It bore armor impervious to armor-piercing shell fire. These self-propelled land-water vehicles were built, beginning on July 22, 1941, in a cooperative effort by the firms of Klöckner-Humboldt-Deutz AG, Werk Magirus, Bodanwerft-Maybach-Zahnradfabrik Friedrichshafen, Krupp-Gruson and Kässbohrer, and the first test model was finished on May 15, 1942. The Krupp-Gruson AG also provided two slightly

modified Panzer IV chassis, which were equipped with water propulsion by C. D. Magirus in Ulm. The power takeoff for water propulsion was connected to the main engine. The armored body was formed like a boat, the vehicle had external measurements of 8250 x 2800 x 2500 mm, and its overall weight was 17 tons.

A complete armored ferry consisted of two self-propelled armored land-water tractors, between which a self-floating ferry deck was attached to ferry equipment. Kässbohrer had also developed a floating trailer for this vehicle.

Since the fighting weight of tanks was increasing quickly, there was no move to develop this interesting design further.

As of October 1944, "Bergepanzer IV" recovery tanks taken from repaired stocks were made available, with 36 of them being delivered to the troops in 1944. In some cases, the troops themselves had rebuilt damaged vehicles with Panzer IV hulls and used them as wreckers.

For towing Panzer I to IV vehicles, including unmanned ones, the AHA/Ag K requested on April 11, 1944 that the firm of Georg Kirsten in Sebnitz, Saxony produce a towing device (towing bars) for tanks. It was supposed to be secured in place so that immobilized tanks could by towed away without difficulty by heavy towing tractors or other tanks. In May and June of 1940, contracts to create a device for transporting Panzer III and IV tanks were given

The first vehicle assembled at the Magirus Works of the Klöckner-Humboldt-Deutz AG. It used a slightly modified Panzer IV running gear. The floating body was impervious to armor-piercing projectiles fired by small arms.

With the "Landwasserschlepper" are the two prototypes of the "Panzerfähre." They remained the only vehicles of this kind.

Panzerfähre (Pz.F.)

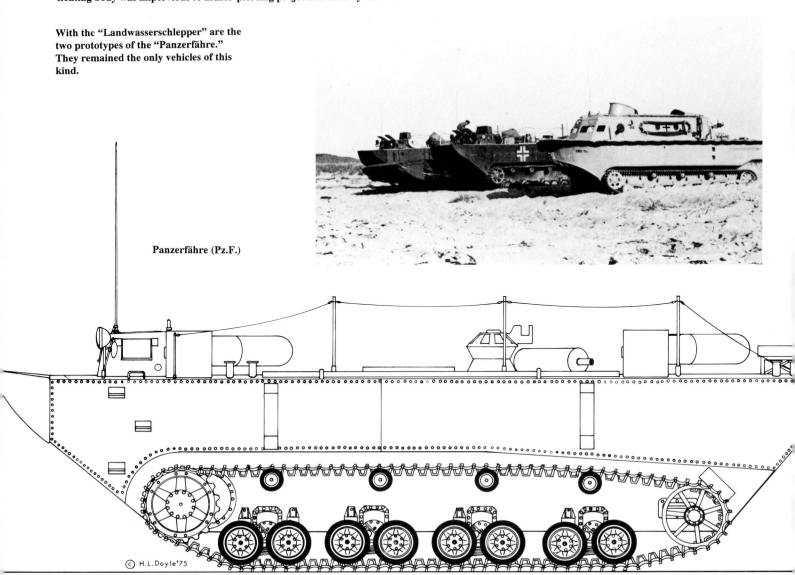

© H.L.Doyle'75

A "Panzerfähre" landing. The registration "111 Z" was that of the governmental district of Ulm, where this vehicle was developed. The first digit 0 indicates that it is a test vehicle.

Left column, top to bottom. The "Pz.F." in the country; the air intake ducts on top are easy to see.

The powerplant package of the ferry shows the Maybach HL 120 engine and the drive train that powered the vehicle in the water.

Here the ferry is going into the water. The floating trailer was built by the Kässbohrer firm.

The ferry in the water. It was built to float in all European waterways.

Two views of the Panzerfähre as it was originally used. A bridge capable of carrying loads of up to 24 tons was suspended between the two vehicles. The calculation of load weights was obviously insufficient, since situations such as that shown in the photograph occurred constantly. The lower photograph shows a prototype bridgelayer with six-roller running gear being ferried.

The two "Panzerfähre" lifting a Maybach HL 120 engine out of a vehicle. The loading tackle could be set up and taken down easily.

Armored trains and trolleys were also equipped with original Panzer IV turrets. Both short and long tank guns were used in them. The photograph above shows an armored trolley being shown to Hitler; below is an armored train, with two turrets, that was captured by the Allies.

by Wa Prüf 6 to the firms of Daimler-Benz and E. F. G. Both devices were delivered in 1941.

The workshop companies were supplied with so-called "large workshop tents" to house six to eight motor vehicles being repaired, including tanks. These tents had already been contracted for to the firm of Salzmann & Co. in Kassel, and were put to good use later for repairing tanks, especially in bad weather.

Conclusion

The Panzerkampfwagen IV, produced in large numbers, was the backbone of the German armored units to the end of the war. Despite its obvious weaknesses in construction and armor and the technical problems caused by shortages of raw materials, The Panzer IV was the most reliable German armored vehicle, and from 1942 on in particular, it was the equal of almost all enemy tanks thanks to its improved armament.

Although in the latter half of the war the troops gave the Panzer IV the nickname of "Rotbart der Hauchdunne" [Redbeard the Thin-Skinned] on account of its weak armor plate. The vehicle was valued by the Panzer companies to the end of the war.

Early in 1943, the General Staff of the Army recommended that the construction of all tanks except the "Panther" and "Tiger" be halted. Generaloberst Heinz Guderian, on the other hand, saw to it that the Panzer IV continued to be built. If the Panzer IV had not continued to be built, then the whole tank production of the German Reich would have consisted of only 25 "Tiger" tanks per month until the "Panther" was ready for series production. The result would necessarily have been a scarcely surmountable crisis for the hard-fighting troops at the front.

APPENDIX I

Specifications of the 7.5 cm KwK L/24

Barrel

Dimensions

Barrel width	74.9 mm
Barrel length	1766.5 mm
in caliber	24
Distance from rear baseplate to	
forward attachment surface	200 mm
Length from forward attachment to muzzle	1566.5 mm
Length of rifled section	1307.5 mm
in caliber	18

Rifling

Number	28
Depth	0.85 mm
Width (average)	4.6 mm
Lands width (average)	3.8 mm

Chamber

Length	259 mm
Diameter at rear	82.1 mm
at front	78.8 mm

Pitch

Beginning	5 degrees 7 min. 45 sec. (35 caliber)
End	6 degrees 53 min. 23 sec. (26 caliber)

Propellant chamber

Length

a. K.Gr. rot Pz. [armor piercing]	198 mm
b. Gr. 34 [high explosive]	183 mm
c. Gr. 38 [HEAT - shaped charge]	183 mm

Volume

a. K.Gr. rot Pz.	1.0 cubic dm
b. Gr. 34	0.9 cubic dm
c. Gr. 38	0.9 cubic dm

Weights

a. K.Gr. rot Pz.	6.8 kg
b. Gr. 34	5.74 kg
c. Gr. 38	4.4 kg

Initial velocity

a. K.Gr. rot Pz.	385 m/sec
b. Gr. 34	420 m/sec
c. Gr. 38	450 m/sec

Gas pressure at +10 degrees Celsius	2400 kg/sq. cm.
Design gas pressure	2800 kg/sq. cm.

Weights

Complete barrel with breech	285 kg
Full barrel	141 kg
Clamp bolt	12 kg
Base without breech	101 kg
Breech with motion apparatus	29.6 kg

Cradle

a. Dimensions

Elevation range	-10 to + 20 degrees
Traverse range	360 degrees
Firing height above ground	1965 mm

Recoil cylinder

Median pressure, 0 degrees elevation,	
recoil 430 mm	4500 kg
Liquid capacity	1.54 liters
Recoil distance, normal	430 mm
Recuperator	
Initial air pressure	25 +/- 2 kg/cm
Liquid capacity	2 liters

b. Weight

Cradle without barrel and base	205 kg
Recoil cylinder	26 kg
Pneumatic recuperator	18 kg
Weight of complete gun	490 kg

APPENDIX 2

Secret
From armor manufacturing
(Details from the report of Reg. Baurat Dipl. Ing. Groner of OKH. Wa. Chef Ing 7)

1. Three types of tank were classified according to armament:
leichte Panzerkampfwagen, 8-10 ton weight, armor to 30 mm, armed with 2 cm weapon plus machine guns;
mittlere Panzerkampfwagen, 18-22 ton weight, 30-50 mm armor, armed with 3.7-5 cm gun plus machine guns;

schwere Panzerkampfwagen, 30-45 ton weight, 50-80 mm armor, armed with 7.5-8.8 cm gun plus machine guns.

Armament, armor and speed are the three chief components that determine the fighting value of a tank. The best combination is the best design.

All tanks and combat vehicles are fully tracked vehicles. Halftrack vehicles are towing tractors, but are still included in the armored vehicle program. Armored (4- and 8-wheel) recon. cars are wheeled vehicles.

2. Technical details

A medium tank includes 15-20,000 individual parts. In its composition, the (18 ton) medium tank is divided into the

Chassis, with engine and running gear, and the Turret with armament.

The chassis is made of treated armor plate; on the outside it carries the running gear, on the inside the power train. All tanks are equipped with a rear engine, gasoline engines exclusively (Diesel engines are for the time being only a possibility for the future). The engine and fighting compartments are separated from each other by a firewall made of armor plate. The engine's power is transferred through a transmission to the front drive wheels. All tanks have exclusively front-wheel drive, as with rear-wheel drive the tracks easily jam and break. The tracks run over road wheels and return rollers. Steering is done by steering brakes, which make it possible to turn the vehicle on the spot.

The road wheels of the tracks are mounted on suspension arms with torsion-bar suspension. This torsion-bar suspension can be located inside the vehicle and thus is very practical for saving space.

3. **The production time** of a medium tank is estimated to be approximately 15,000 round work hours, of which 5000 are used for primary preparation and 10,000 by the sub-contractors (including weapons and optics). Production is divided among

a. Production of the hull, which is made by heavy industry, the working, handling and welding of the raw material (alloy steel), which requires very special experience and large- scale facilities.

b. Production of the tracks, which requires facilities for casting and forging steel (drop-forging and blacksmithing). c. Engine production, exclusively of Maybach engines (300 HP), because these are the most reliable on the basis of special experience in large-engine construction. Licensed production firms are included on an individual basis.

d. Transmission production, primarily by the Zahnradfabrik Friedrichshafen.

e. Small parts are delivered primarily by the automobile industry.

f. Weapons and optics are delivered by the appropriate industries.

g. The assembly works put all of these together.

For evaluating the production facilities, the following should be kept in mind:

For the hull, only heavy industry can be considered, beginning with, in order, steel mills, rolling mills, alloying plants and welding facilities.

The raw material is alloy steel; its analysis is a secret. Electric ovens to a capacity of 35 tons. The four-sided steel blocks are worked on all sides, to prevent tearing and lumping during rolling, before they reach the rolling mill. They are worked primarily on cold lines; later the warmed block is to be worked (to save time).

The rolling mills for the 30-80 mm armor plate are financed exclusively by the OKH. The rolling process is as follows:

Warming – rolling – air-cooling, which requires much space for sand beds! – annealing (large annealing ovens) – aligning on rolling-aligning machines and aligning presses, automatic cutting (to 1/10 accuracy) – fitting the pieces to each other (presses must be operated mechanically), heat-treatment again (oil quenching, with tension, against stretching). The surface hardening (grisogenic process) is applied to the front plates. The sheets are then assembled for welding. Welding is done in large frames of 8-10 x 4-5 x 5-meter dimensions, that can be rotated to provide easier access to the welder. Cast steel and drop-forged pieces are welded into the hull, and thus it is ready for delivery to the assembly plant.

Tracks: Cast and forged tracks are used. Only unlubricated tracks are used on tanks, while towing tractors use lubricated tracks because of their higher speed. Cast track components of hardened cast steel can no longer be prepared, therefore unlubricated tracks. Number of links 80 to 100 per track, one set = two tracks. Electric steel casting works with large casting and forming surfaces for mass production, production lines are needed. One track link weighs 5-6 kg, precise preparation! Wall thicknesses to only 4 mm. Tolerances to tenths of a millimeter are required. Machines and large-scale cleaning facilities are necessary.

Assembly of tracks is then done at the foundry to decrease transport.

Track wear amounts to 200-300% of newly-made material,
hence the great importance of firms providing spare parts.

Some 10 to 12 assembly firms for tanks exist at this time; subcontractor firms in France presently deliver up to half of the total track needs. Only finishing firms with large areas for hulls, engines, raw components, finished components can be considered for assembly.

For example: Mounting facilities with 75,000 square meters of surface area with ten halls of 5000 to 20,000 square meters. Therefore capacity expansion is only possible with such facilities. Main halls with cranes up to 60 tons capacity for entire vehicles.

The machine layout of the finishing firms must be universal, avoid too many special machines, as tank production is too new and thus constantly in flux. For example, 10 to 12 different types of the Panzer III are currently being built.

In seven months America built a tank factory from the ground up, and it produced 100 tanks per month (specific types). The tank did not prove itself and the factory had to cease production. Thus: universal, quickly convertible finishing facilities are always preferable.

The working of the external surfaces of the hull for attached parts requires carousel turning banks up to a diameter of 3.5 meters.

The installation of vitally important components and the final assembly require assembly lines with step-by-step procedures, with the vehicle lying on its bottom. The supply lines run vertically to the main line. A capacity of 100 tanks in two shifts requires some 1000 to 1200 machine tools of the medium and large types.

Running-in finished vehicles is done in climatically controlled cells (for Africa) and in the open air.

Increasing production is overseen and carried out by Sonderausschuss VI. One representative of each production firm is a member of it. Differences in production presently exist to 100%; therefore exchanging experience in the Sonderausschuss is urgently needed.

Concerning materials: replacement materials are also utilized. At this time, German vehicles utilize only 1/3 to 1/4 of the quantity of non-ferrous metals in comparison to foreign tank types. High-grade steels are used, but without a high percentage of high-priced additives, these are the results of the latest research work in steel production. The only disadvantages are the difficulties of working these new steels.

Design work is carried out in a coordination department under the supervision of the Heeres Waffenamt. Designers from all production firms are represented. The preparation of powertrain drawings requires 6 to 7 months just for the component suppliers, not including engine production firms (100 to 1500 drawings).

The work force of the component suppliers consists of up to 80% skilled and unskilled work forces. Women are employed less often, because the component weights are too great.

Spare-part delivery had to be developed particularly without disturbing firms in new production. Wear = 30% of the cost of new production. The main share is in motor, running-gear and transmission parts; track wear is 200 to 300%. The numerous types and series cause difficulties. Spare-parts firms deliver to the spare-parts storage facility in Magdeburg.

3/25/1942 Signed

APPENDIX 3

Investigation of Space and Weight Savings in the 400 HP MB 809 Diesel Engine
(according to notes in the files of Director Mr. Nallinger of 10/31/1938)

1. As opposed to the previously expected 400 HP at n = 2200 of the medium-version MB 809 (21.7 liters) with some 3.0 kg/HP (cast iron individual cylinders), total weight 1250 kg,
2. While maintaining the required specification of 400 HP, a weight reduction and shortening of the motor was achieved,
 a. by using individual cylinders of steel with welded-on cooling jackets,
 b. with a 2-liter reduction of the engine displacement to 19.7 liters, by increasing the engine speed to n = 2400, 400 HP was achieved, whereby the unit weight amounted to only 2.7-2.8 kg/HP (1120 kg), and the motor was shortened by 100 mm.

The MB 809 version that was finally introduced, with 17.5 liters displacement, produced 360 HP at n = 2400 rpm and weighed only 820 kg, representing a unit weight of only 2.27 kg/HP.

The use of steel cylinders achieved not only a reduction in weight and length, but also the possibility of installing larger valves (– which alone allowed the attainment of higher power –), plus the great advantage of unqualified safety against cylinder-head breakage, which must always be considered with cast iron cylinders.

APPENDIX 4

High Command of the Army Berlin W 35, December 23, 1938 Bb. No. 12390/38 geh. Wa Prüf 6 (1c) Tirpitzufer 72-76

Design Guidelines for the Development of Diesel Engines for Tanks

1. In close cooperation with the O.K.W., Wa Prüf 6, Diesel engines are to be developed for installation in tanks.
2. Work processes and engine design remain free, with the acceptance of the prescribed norms and considerable avoidance of materials in short supply to be taken for granted.
3. The highest power outputs of the various engines, which are to be developed for especially light weight and smallest dimensions, are as follows:
 a. 150 HP
(Stamp: Secret according to 88 RStGB)
 b. 200 HP
 c. 250 HP
 d. 320 HP
 e. 400 HP
 f. 650 HP

4. In the enclosures, the greatest allowable dimensions of each engine, with its position and running speed, can be found.
5. The engine is to be housed in the engine compartment, along with all its attached parts, plus air filters, cooling system, and storage batteries, as well as a fuel supply sufficient for the engine to run at full speed for five hours. Details, particularly as regards the air filters, ventilating and cooling systems, are to be determined together with the O. K. W. Wa Prüf 6.
6. The dry power-to-weight ratio of the engine including all attached parts but without cooling systems, clutch and clutch housing, may not exceed 4.5 kg per HP for the smallest size, and must be correspondingly smaller for larger sizes.
7. Highest power is understood to mean the greatest sustained performance of the engine, which it produces with all integral parts exclusive of the cooling system over 100 hours of steady running without having to be overhauled afterward.

8. The torque of the engine must not decrease more than 10% of its maximum value within the operating range of engine speed, which is to extend from the highest engine speed to one third thereof.

9. The engine must attain the required performance in trouble-free operation while using a fuel produced in this country, with the octane rating of 50.

10. All parts that require service, such as nozzles, pumps, valves, filters, oil pumps, must be sufficiently accessible in the engine compartment and on the engine, for which the agreement of the O.K.W., Wa Prüf 6, is to be obtained.

11. Parts which are strongly exposed to wear must be located where they are easy to replace.

12. The engine must be capable of being started without trouble with an electric starter in warm weather and with a special starter in cold temperatures to -15 degrees Celsius. In all engines, the installation of 800- to 1000- or 1300-watt generators, according to requirements, must be provided for.

13. The type acceptance of the engines will take place according to the requirements applying to them, in connection with a test of adherence to the existing requirements.

14. For production engines, the manufacturing firm is obligated to provide a guarantee of their performance for a distance of 5000 km covered by the vehicle.

15. Firms that undertake to develop one or more Diesel engines for tanks in cooperation and at the expense of the O.K.W. commit themselves by signing a special developmental contract to allowing other firms to build the engines or their parts at no charge.

APPENDIX 5

Wa Prüf (B) 1/W-2b Hillersleben, March 23, 1944
Comparison
of German tanks with the new Russian T 34-85 and JS 122 tanks

Compared are the penetrating ranges of the German

Pz.Kpfw. Panzer IV with 7.5 cm KwK 40
Panther with 7.5 cm KwK 42
Tiger 1 with 8.8 cm KwK 36
Tiger 1 with 8.8 cm KwK 43, and
Tiger 2 with 8.8 cm KwK 43

with the new Russian T 34-85 and JS 122 tanks with the penetrating ranges of the two Russian tanks as opposed to the German tanks listed above.

Since no test firing results are available, all penetration figures have been calculated. The calculations have been based on the armor strengths and plate angles stated in Appendix 2.

According to information available here, the Russian 8.5 cm gun (L.51) fires an armor piercing projectile that weighs 9.2 kg at an initial velocity of 792 m/sec and the Russian 12,2 cm gun fires an armor piercing projectile with a weight of 25 kg at an initial velocity of 800 m/sec. The penetration curves of the Russian weapons used here are taken from Russian information. All the penetration curves were available to a distance of only 2000 meters and had to be estimated to distances up to 3500 meters.

The penetrating performance for a combat distance of 1000 meters at a 60-degree angle of impact are stated here:

7.5 cm KwK 40 with 7.5 cm Pz. Gr. 39 -99 mm
7.5 cm KwK 42 with 7.5 cm Pz. Gr. 39/42 -138 mm
8.8 cm KwK 36 with 8.8 cm Pz. Gr. 39 -120 mm
8.8 cm KwK 43 with 8.8 cm Pz. Gr. 39/43 -202 mm
8.5 cm KwK (r) with 8.5 cm Pz. Gr. (r) -109 mm
12.2 cm KwK (r) with 12.2 cm Pz. Gr. (r) -134 mm

These calculations are based on an assumed angle of impact of 60 degrees from the horizontal. The armor material was all equated to the plate material for test firing; in the case of cast steel, a plate strength decreased by 14% was calculated. For strongly arched armored parts (such as weapon mounts), an angle of inclination of 60 degrees was assumed.

The accuracy of the individual weapons was not taken into consideration in this comparison.

A compilation of the penetration ranges calculated for the individual surfaces of the tanks is included in Appendix 1.

In brief, it can be said that the

Panzer IV
is far inferior to the T 34-85 and JS 122.

The Panther
is far superior to the T 34-85 for frontal fire, approximately equal for side and rear fire, superior to the JS for frontal fire and inferior for side and rear fire.

The Tiger 1 with KwK 36
is superior to the T 34-85 and inferior to the Js 122.

The Tiger 1 with KwK 43
is superior to both the T 34-85 and the JS 122.

The Tiger 2
is far superior to the T 34-85 and the JS 122.

Signed

APPENDIX 6

The form of payment for weapons contracted for by the Army High Command can be seen from the two original documents shown in this appendix. These so-called Armed Forces Certificates of Indebtedness were intended to cover the costs that industry and trade incurred in filling contracts. In the example at hand, a payment was made to the A. Fross-Büssing KG of Vienna, which is known to have delivered turret and ventilator drives for armored vehicles during the war.

Oberkommando des Heeres
(Ch H Rüst u. B d E)
58 c 10 10 Wa Z 2 IIIa
Kontroll-Nr. 3145

Berlin W 35, den   8. 5.   19 42
Tirpitzufer 72-76

— 1 Anlage —

Betr.: Ausstellung eines Wehrmacht-verpflichtungsscheines.

Firma   A. Fross-Büssing K.G.,

in   W i e n
Nordwestbahnstr. 53

Auf Grund Ihres an das Oberkommando des Heeres (Ch H Rüst u. B d E) — Wa J Rü   (WuG 6)   — gerichteten Antrages wird Ihnen hiermit ein Wehrmachtverpflichtungsschein (Nr.   03145   ) in Höhe von

2.295.000,-- RM

übersandt für den Ihnen erteilten Kriegsauftrag Nr.   217-0036/41, Best. Ag. K/M
14/41,54

Es wird gebeten, den Eingang des W.-V.-Sch. zu bestätigen.

Die Einlösung des W.-V.-Sch. an dem darauf angegebenen Fälligkeitstage ist nur gewährleistet, wenn der W.-V.-Sch. **10 Tage vor Fälligkeit** beim Heereswaffenamt (Wa Z 2 IIIa), Berlin W 35, Tirpitzufer 72-76, eingeht. Es wird gebeten, bei Weitergabe des W.-V.-Sch. an eine Bank, Girokasse oder ähnl. hierauf besonders hinzuweisen.

J. A.

452. 1. 42. Dr T

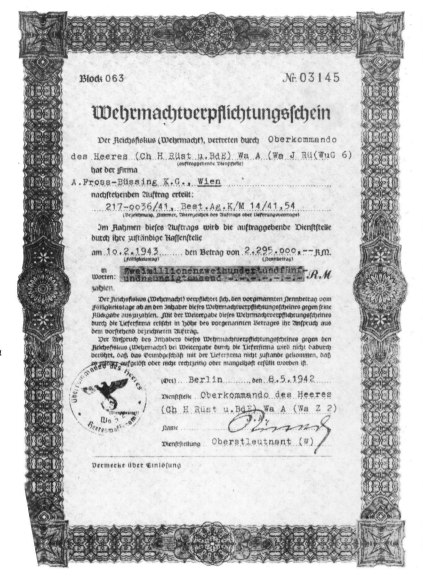

153

Vehicle Designation	Panzerkampfwagen IV (Vs.Kfz.622)	Panzerkampfwagen IV (Vs.Kfz.622)	Panzerkampfwagen IV (Vs.Kfz.622)
Ausf.	A	B	C
Type	1/BW	2/BW	3/BW
Manufacturer	Krupp-Grusonwerk AG	Krupp-Grusonwerk AG	Krupp-Grusonwerk AG
Years built	1937-1938	1938	1938-1939
Information source	D 653/1, 1Nov42	D 653/1, 1Nov42	D 653/5, 10Nov41

Engine	Maybach HL 108 TR	Maybach HL 120 TR	Maybach HL 120 TRM*
Cylinders	60-degree V12	60-degree V12	60-degree V12
Bore x stroke (mm)	100 x 115	105 x 115	105 x 115
Displacement (cc)	10838	11867	11867
Compression ratio	6.5 : 1	6.5 : 1	6.5 : 1
RPM normal/maximum	2600/3000	2600/3000	2600/3000
Horsepower	230/250	265/300	265/300
Valves	Dropped, 1 camshaft per cylinder head		
Crankshaft	7 roller bearings	7 roller bearings	7 roller bearings
Carburetors	2 Solex 40 JFF II	2 Solex 40 JFF II	2 Solex 40 JFF II
Firing order	1-8-5-10-3-7-6-11-2-9-4-12	1-12-5-8-3-10-6-7-2-11-4-9	1-12-5-8-3-10-6-7-2-11-4-9
Starter	Bosch BNG 4/24 CRS 178	Bosch BNG 4/24	Bosch BNG 4/24
Generator	2 Bosch GQL 300/12-900	2 Bosch GTLN 600/12-1500	2 Bosch GTLN 600/12-1500
Batteries	4 6-volt 105 Ah	4 6-volt 105 Ah	4 6-volt 105 Ah
Fuel pumps	2 Solex	2 mechanical	2 mechanical
Coolant	Water	Water	Water

Clutch	Dry 3-plate	Dry 3-plate	Dry 3-plate
Transmission	ZF SFG 75 shear	ZF SSG 76 Aphon	ZF SSG 76 Aphon
Speeds forward\reverse	5/1	6/1	6/1
Drive wheels	Front	Front	Front
Axle ratio	1:4	1:3.23	1:3.23
Top speed	30 km/hr	35 km/hr	35 km/hr
Range on/off road	140/90 km	140/90 km	140/90 km
Steering	Krupp-Wilson clutch	Krupp-Wilson clutch	Krupp-Wilson clutch
Turning circle (m)	5.92	5.92	5.92

Suspension	Quarter-elliptic longitudinal leaf springs, 4 trucks, two per spring		
Lubrication	High-pressure	High-pressure	High-pressure
Brake system	Fried.Krupp AG	Fried.Krupp AG	Fried.Krupp AG
Brake operation	Mechanical	Mechanical	Mechanical
Brake type	External	External	External
Brake effect on	Drive wheels	Drive wheels	Drive wheels
Running gear	Road wheels + return rollers	Road wheels + return rollers	Road wheels + return rollers
Road wheel size	470 x 75-660	470 x 75-660	470 x 75-660
Track base (mm)	2390	2390	2390
Track length (mm)	3720	3720	3720
Track width (mm)	360	360	360
Links per track	101	101	101
Track type			
Ground clearance (mm)	400	400	400
Overall length (mm)	5920	5870	5870
Overall width (mm)	2830	2830	2830
Overall height (mm)	2680	2680	2680
Ground pressure kg/sq cm	0.69	0.7	0.75
Fighting weight (kg)	17300	17700	18500
Crew	5	5	5
Fuel consumption (liters/100 km on/off road)	318/500	330/500	330/500
Fuel capacity (liters)	139 + 109 + 205 = 453	470 (3 tanks)	470 (3 tanks)

Hull armor: front (mm)	14.5	30	30
sides (mm)	14.5	14.5	14.5
rear (mm)	14.5	20	20
Turret armor: front (mm)	20	20	30
sides (mm)	20	20	20
rear (mm)	20	20	20
Climbing (degrees)	35	30	30
Step (mm)	710	600	600
Fording (mm)	800	800	800
Crossing (mm)	2600	2300	2300
Weapons, primary	1 7.5 cm KwK L/24 (122)**	1 7.5 cm KwK L/24 (80)	1 7.5 cm KwK L/24 (80)
secondary	2 MG 34 (3000)	1 MG 34 (2700)	1 MG 34 (2700)
Notes	** ammunition in () Munitionsvorrat		* The first 40 with Maybach HL 120 TR engines.

Vehicle Designation	Panzerkampfwagen IV (Sd.Kfz.161)	Panzerkampfwagen IV (Sd.Kfz.161)	Panzerkampfwagen IV (Sd.Kfz.161)
Ausf.	D	E	F1
Type	4/ & 5/BW	6/BW	7/BW
Manufacturer	Krupp-Grusonwerk AG	Krupp-Grusonwerk AG	Krupp-Grusonwerk AG
Years built	1939-1941	1940-1941	1941-1942
Information source	D 653/9, 10Jan39	D 653/25, 25Sep39	D 653/7, 1Apr42

	D	E	F1
Engine		Maybach HL 120 TRM	
Cylinders		60-degree V-12	
Bore x stroke (mm)		105 x 115	
Displacement (cc)		11867	
Compression ratio		6.5 : 1	
RPM, normal/maximum		2600/3000	
Horsepower		265/300	
Valves		Dropped, 1 camshaft per cylinder head	
Crankshaft		7 bearings	
Carburetors		2 Solex 40 JFF II	
Firing order		1-12-5-8-3-10-6-7-2-11-4-9	
Starter		Bosch BNG 4/24	
Generators		2 Bosch GTLN 600/12-1500	
Batteries	4 6-volt, 105 Ah	4 6-volt, 105 Ah	4 12-volt, 105 Ah
Fuel pumps		2 mechanical, 1 electric	
Coolant		Water	

	D	E	F1
Clutch		F & S La 120/HDA dry 3-plate	
Transmission		ZF SSG 76 Aphon	
Speeds		6 forward, 1 reverse	
Drive wheels		Front	
Axle ratio		1 : 3.23	
Top speed km/hr	42	42	42
Range on/off road	210/130	200/125	200\130
Steering		Krupp-Wilson clutch	
Turning circle (m)		5.92	

	D	E	F1
Springs		Quarter-elliptic longitudinal leaf, 4 trucks, 2 trucks per spring	
Lubrication		High-pressure	
Brake system		Fried.Krupp AG	
Brake operation		Mechanical	
Brake type		External	
Brake effect on		Drive wheels	
Running gear		Road wheels + return rollers	
Road wheel size		470 x 75-660	
Track base (mm)	2400	2400	2450
Track length (mm)	3720	3720	3520
Track width (mm)	360	360	400
Links per track	101	101	99
Type of track			Kgs 61/400/120
Ground clearance (mm)	400	400	400
Overall length (mm)	5920	5920	5920
Overall width (mm)	2840	2840	2880
Overall height (mm)	2680	2680	2680
Ground pressure kg/sq. cm	0.77	0.79	0.79
Fighting weight (kg)	20000	21000	22300
Crew	5	5	5
Fuel consumption (liters/100 km on/off road)	250/350	250/350	250/350
Fuel capacity (liters)		140 + 110 + 220 = 470	

	D	E	F1
Hull armor front (mm)	30	30 + 30	50
sides (mm)	20	20 + 20	30
rear (mm)	20	20	20
Turret armor front (mm)	30	30	50
sides (mm)	20	20	30
rear (mm)	20	20	30
Climbing (degrees)	30	30	30
Step (mm)	600	600	600
Fording (mm)	1000	1000	1000
Crossing (mm)	2300	2300	2300
Weapons, primary	1 7.5 cm KwK L/24 (80)	1 7.5 cm KwK L/24 (80)	1 7.5 cm KwK L/24 (80)
secondary	2 MG 34 (2700)	2 MG 34 (2700)	2 MG 34 (3192)
Notes			

Vehicle Designation	Panzerkampfwagen IV (Sd.Kfz.161)	Panzerkampfwagen IV (Sd.Kfz.161/1)	Panzerkampfwagen IV (Sd.Kfz.161/2)
Ausf.	F2	G	H
Type	7/BW	7/BW	BW
Manufacturer	Krupp, Nibelungenwerke, Vomag	Krupp, Nibelungenwerke, Vomag	Krupp, Nibelungenwerke, Vomag
Years built	1942	1942-1943	1943-1944
Information source	D 653/7, 1Apr42	D 653/50, 1Jul44	D 653/50, 1Jul44
Engine	Maybach HL 120 TRM		
Cylinders	60-degree V12		
Bore x stroke (mm)	105 x 115		
Displacement (cc)	11867		
Compression ratio	6.5 : 1		
RPM normal/maximum	2600/3000		
Horsepower	265/300		
Valves	Dropped, 1 camshaft per cylinder head		
Crankshaft	7 roller bearings		
Carburetors	2 Solex 40 JFF II		
Firing order	1-12-5-8-3-10-6-7-2-11-4-9		
Starter	Bosch BNG 4/24		
Generators	2 Bosch GTLN 600/12-1500		
Batteries	4 12-volt, 105 Ah		
Fuel pumps	2 mechanical, 1 electric		
Coolant	Water		
Clutch	F & S La 120/HDA dry 3-plate		
Transmission	ZF SSG 76 Aphon	ZF SSG 76 Aphon	ZF SSG 76 Aphon
Speeds forward/reverse	6/1	6/1	6/1
Drive wheels	Front	Front	Front
Axle ratio	1 : 3.23	1 : 3.23	1 : 3.23
Top speed km/hr	40	40	38
Range on/off road	210/130	210/130	210/130
Steering type	Krupp-Wilson clutch		
Turning circle (m)	5.92		
Springs	Quarter-elliptic longitudinal leaf, 4 trucks, 2 trucks per spring		
Lubrication	High-pressure		
Brake system	Fried.Krupp AG		
Brake operation	Mechanical		
Brake type	External		
Brake effect on	Drive wheels		
Running gear	Road wheels + return rollers		
Road wheel size	470 x 75-660		
Track base (mm)	2450 (Eastern tracks: 2650)		
Track length (mm)	3520		
Track width (mm)	400		
Links per track	99		
Track type	Kgs 61/400/120		
Ground clearance (mm)	400		
Overall length (mm)	6630	6630	7015
Overall width (mm)	2280 (3192 with eastern tracks, 3330 with aprons)		
Overall height (mm)	2680		
Ground pressure kg/sq. cm	0.84	0.84	0.89
Fighting weight (kg)	23600	23500	25999
Crew	5	5	5
Fuel consumption (liters/100 km)	250 on/350 off road		
Fuel capacity	470 (3 tanks)		
Hull armor front (mm)	50	50	80
sides (mm)	30	30	30
rear (mm)	20	20	20
Turret armor front (mm)	50	50	50
sides (mm)	30	30	30
rear (mm)	30	30	30
Climbing (degrees)	30	30	30
Step (mm)	600	600	600
Fording (mm)	1000	1000	1200
Crossing (mm)	2200	2200	2200
Weapons, primary	1 7.5 cm KwK 40 L/43 (87)	1 7.5 cm KwK 40 L/43 (87)	1 7.5 cm KwK 40 L/48 (87)
secondary	2 MG 34 (3192)	2 MG 34 (2250)	2 MG 34 (3150)
Notes	[blank, * included in listing]		

Vehicle Designation	Panzerkampfwagen IV (Sd.Kfz.161/2)	Jagdpanzer IV (Sd.Kfz.162)	Sturmgeschütz IV (L/48) [blank]
Ausf.	J	F	[blank]
Type	BW	7/BW	BW
Manufacturer	Nibelungenwerke	Vomag	Krupp-Grusonwerk AG
Years built	1944-1945	1944	1944-1945
Information source	D 653/50, 1Jul44	D 653/39. 15Sep44	Handbook WaA, G 340 III

Engine		Maybach HL 120 TRM	
Cylinders		60-degree V12	
Bore x stroke (mm)		105 x 115	
Displacement (cc) 11867			
Compression ratio		6.5 : 1	
RPM normal/maximum		2600/3000	
Horsepower		265/300	
Valves		Dropped, 1 camshaft per cylinder head	
Crankshaft		7 roller bearings	
Carburetors		2 Solex 40 JFF II	
Firing order		1-12-5-8-3-10-6-7-2-11-4-9	
Starter		Bosch BNG 4/24	
Generators		2 Bosch GTLN 600/12-1500	
Batteries		4 12-volt, 105 Ah	
Fuel pumps		2 mechanical, 1 electric	
Coolant		Water	

Clutch		F & S La 120/HDA three-plate dry	
Transmission		ZF SSG 76 Aphon	
Speeds		6 forward, 1 reverse	
Drive wheels		Front	
Axle ratio		1 : 3.23	
Top speed km/hr	38	40	38
Range on/off road	320/210	210/130	320/210
Steering		Krupp-Wilson clutch	
Turning circle		5.92 meters	

Springs		Longitudinal quarter-elliptic, 4 trucks, 2 trucks per spring	
Lubrication		High-pressure	
Brake system		Fried.Krupp AG	
Brake operation		Mechanical	
Brake type		External	
Brake effect on		Drive wheels	
Running gear		Road wheels and return rollers	
Road wheel size		470 x 75-660	
Track base (mm)		2450 (2460 with eastern tracks)	
Track length (mm)		3520	
Track width (mm)		400	
Track links		99	
Track type		Kgs 61/400/120	
Ground clearance (mm)		400	
Overall length (mm)	7015	6850	6700
Overall width (mm)	2880 (3300 with aprons)	3170 (3210 with eastern tracks)	2950
Overall height (mm)	2680	1850	2200
Ground pressure (kg/sq. cm)	0.89	0.86 (0.62 with eastern tracks)	0.8
Fighting weight (kg)	25000	24000	23000
Crew	5	4 (or 5)	4
Fuel consumption (liters/100 km on/off road)	250/350	250/350	250/350
Fuel capacity (liters)	680 (4 tanks)	470 (3 tanks)	430

Hull armor front (mm)	80	Body front 60	Body front 80
sides (mm)	30	sides 40	sides 30
rear (mm)	20	rear 30	rear 20
Turret armor front (mm)	50		
sides (mm)	30		
rear (mm)	30		
Climbing (degrees)	30	30	30
Step (mm)	600	600	600
Fording (mm)	1200	1000	1200
Crossing (mm)	2200	2200	2200
Weapons, primary	1 7.5 cm KwK 40 L/48 (87)	1 7.5 cm Pak 39 L/48 (79)	1 7.5 cm StuK 40 L/48 (63)
secondary	2 MG 34 (3150)	1 MG 42	1 MG 34

Vehicle Designation	Panzer IV/70 (V) (Sd.Kfz.162/1)	Sturmpanzer (Sd.Kfz.166)	3.7 cm Flak 43 auf Sfl Pz.Kpfw.IV "Möbelwagen"
Ausf.	–	–	–
Type	BW	BW	BW
Manufacturer	Vomag	Deutsche Eisenwerke AG \	
Years built	1944-1945	1943-1945	1944-1945
Information source	Handbook WaA, G 356	Handbook WaA, G 344	Handbook WaA, 318

Engine		Maybach HL 120 TRM	Maybach HL 120 TRM 112
Cylinders		60-degree V12	60-degree V12
Bore x stroke (mm)		105 x 115	105 x 115
Displacement (cc)		11867	11867
Compression ratio		6.2-6.5 : 1	6.2-6.5 : 1
RPM normal/maximum		2600/3000	2800
Horsepower		265/300	272
Valves		Dropped, 1 camshaft per cylinder head	
Crankshaft		7 roller bearings	
Carburetors		2 Solex 40 JFF II	
Firing order		1-12-5-8-3-10-6-7-2-11-4-9	
Starter		Bosch BNG 4/24	
Generator		Bosch GTLN 600/12-1500	
Batteries		4 12-volt, 105 Ah	
Fuel pumps		2 mechanical, 1 electric	
Coolant		Water	

Clutch		F & S La 120/HDA dry three-plate	
Transmission		ZF SSG 76 Aphon	
Speeds		6 forward, 1 reverse	
Drive wheels		Front	
Axle ratio		1 : 3.23	
Top speed (km/hr)	35	40	38
Range on/off road	210/130	210/130	200/130
Steering		Krupp-Wilson clutch	
Turning circle (meters)		5.92	

Springs		Quarter-elliptic leaf, 4 trucks, 2 per spring	
Lubrication		High-pressure	
Brake system		Fried.Krupp AG	
Brake operation		mechanical	
Brake type		External	
Brake effect on		Drive wheels	
Running gear		Road wheels + return rollers	
Road wheel size		470 x 75-660	
Track base (mm)		2450	
Track length (mm)		3520	
Track width (mm)		400	
Links per track		99	
Track type		Kgs 61/400/120	
Ground clearance (mm)		400	
Overall length (mm)	8500	5930	4610
Overall width (mm)	3170 (3210 with eastern tracks)	2880 (3186 with eastern tracks)	4610
Overall height (mm)	1850	2520	2700
Ground pressure kg/sq. cm	0.9	0.98	0.89
Fighting weight (kg)	25800	28200	25000
Crew	4 (or 5)	5	5
Fuel consumption (liters/100 km on/off road)	220/360	225/360	220/360
Fuel capacity (liters)	470 (3 tanks)	470 (3 tanks)	470 (3 tanks)

Hull armor front (mm)	80	50 + 50	80
sides (mm)	30	20 + 20	30
rear (mm)	20	20	20
Superstructure front (mm)	80	100	25
sides (mm)	40	50	2 x 10, later 20
rear (mm)	30	30	2 x 10, later 20
Climbing (degrees)	30	30	30
Step (mm)	600	600	600
Fording (mm)	1000	1000	1000
Crossing (mm)	2200	2200	2200
Weapons, primary	1 7.5 cm Pak 42 (L/70) (55)	1 15 cm StuH 43 (L/12) (38)	1 3.7 cm Flak 43 (416)
secondary	[blank]	1 MG 34 (600)	–
Notes			similar prototype with 2 cm Flakvierling 38

Vehicle designation	Flakpanzer IV, 2 cm "Wirbelwind"	Flakpanzer IV, 3.7 cm "Ostwind"	leichter Flakpanzer IV (3 cm) "Kugelblitz" (prototype)
Ausf.	–	–	–
Type	BW	BW	BW
Manufacturer	Ostbau	Deutsche Eisenwerke AG	Daimler-Benz AG
Years built	1944-1945	1944-1945	1945
Information source	Handbook WaA, G 317	D 653/46, 20Nov44	PB. 77699, 27Aug45

Engine	Maybach HL 120 TRM 112
Cylinders	60-degree V12
Bore x stroke (mm)	105 x 115
Displacement (cc)	11867
Compression ratio	6.2-6.5 : 1
RPM normal/maximum	2800
Horsepower	272
Valves	Dropped, 1 camshaft per cylinder head
Crankshaft	7 roller bearings
Carburetors	2 Solex 40 KFF II 2
Firing order	1-12-5-8-3-10-6-7-2-11-4-9
Starter	Bosch BNG 4/24
Generator	Bosch GTLN 600/12-1500
Batteries	4 12-volt, 105 Ah
Fuel pumps	2 mechanical, 1 electric
Coolant	Water

Clutch	F & S La 120/HDA dry 3-plate
Transmission	ZF SSG 76 Aphon
Speeds	6 forward, 1 reverse
Drive wheels	Front
Axle ratio	1 : 3.23
Top speed km/hr	38
Range on/off road	210/130
Steering	Krupp-Wilson clutch
Turning circle (meters)	5.92

Springs	Longitudinal quarter-elliptic leaf, 4 trucks, 2 per spring		
Lubrication	High-pressure		
Brake system	Fried.Krupp AG		
Brake operation	Mechanical		
Brake type	Exterior		
Brake effect on	Drive wheels		
Running gear	Road wheels and return rollers		
Road wheel size	470 x 75-660		
Track base (mm)	2450 (2620 with eastern tracks)		
Track length (mm)	3520		
Track width (mm)	400		
Links per track	99		
Track type	Kgs 61/400/120		
Ground clearance (mm)	400		
Overall length (mm)	5920	5920	5920
Overall width (mm)	2950	2950	2950
Overall height (mm)	2760	2750	2950
Ground pressure kg/sq. cm	0.8	0.89	0.89
Fighting weight (kg)	22000	25000	25000
Crew	5	7	5
Fuel consumption (liters/100 km on/off road)	220/360		
Fuel capacity (liters)	470 (3 tanks)		

Hull armor front (mm)	80	80	80
sides (mm)	30	30	30
rear (mm)	20	20	20
Turret armor front (mm)	16	25	25
sides (mm)	16	25	25
rear (mm)	16	25	25
Climbing (degrees)	30	30	30
Step (mm)	600	600	600
Fording (mm)	1200	1200	1200
Crossing (mm)	2200	2200	2200
Armament primary	1 2 cm Flakvierling 38 (3200)	1 3.7 cm Flak 43 (L/60) (1000)	1 3 cm Flakzwilling MK 103/38 (1200)
secondary	1 MG 34 (1350)	1 MG 34	1 MG 42
Notes			

Vehicle designation	8.8 cm Pak 43/1 (L/71) auf Fgst. Pz. Kpfw.III/IV (Sf) "Nashorn" (Sd.Kfz.164)	15 cm Pz.Haub. 18/1 auf Fgst. Pz. Kpfw.III/IV (Sf) "Hummel (Sd.Kfz.165)	leichte Feldhaubitze (Sfl) "Heuschrecke 10"-Prototype
Ausf.	–	–	–
Type			
Manufacturer	Deutsche Eisenwerke AG	Deutsche Eisenwerke AG	Fried.Krupp AG
Years built	1943-1945	1943-1945	1942-1943
Information source	D 653/42, 15Oct43	D 653/43, 15Oct43	Report 1269/43 g, 22Feb43
Engine		Maybach HL 120 TRM, Type A	Maybach HL 90/100
Cylinders		60-degree V12	60-degree V12
Bore x stroke (mm)		105 x 115	100 x 106
Displacement (cc)		11867	9990
Compression ratio		6.2-6.5 : 1	6.5 : 1
RPM normal, maximum		2600/3000	4000
Horsepower		265/300	400
Valves		Dropped, 1 camshaft per cylinder head	
Crankshaft		7 roller bearings	
Carburetors		2 Solex 40 JFF II	
Firing order		1-12-5-8-3-10-6-7-2-11-4-9	
Starter		Bosch BNG 4/24	
Generator		Bosch GTLN 600/12-1500	
Batteries		2 12-volt, 105 Ah	
Fuel pumps		2 mechanical, 1 electric	
Coolant		Water	
Clutch		F & S La 120 HDA dry 3-plate	
Transmission		ZF SSG 77 Aphon	
Speeds		6 forward, 1 reverse	
Drive wheels		Front	
Axle ratio		1 : 4	
Top speed km/hr	40	42	45
Range on/off road	260/130	215/130	300/150
Steering		Daimler-Benz-Wilson clutch	
Turning circle		5.92 meters	
Springs		Longitudinal quarter-elliptic, 4 trucks, 2 per spring	
Lubrication		High-pressure	
Brake system		Fried.Krupp AG	
Brake operation		Mechanical	
Brake type		External	
Brakes work on		Drive wheels	
Running gear		Road wheels + return rollers	
Road wheel size		470 x 75-660	
Track base (mm)		2450	
Track length (mm)	3800 minus pressure ring		3520
Track width (mm)	400		400
Links per track	104		108
Track type			
Ground clearance (mm)	400	400	400
Overall length (mm)	8440 (7260 minus gun)	7170	6000
Overall width (mm)	2950 (3176 + eastern tracks)	2970 (3260 + eastern tracks)	3000
Overall height (mm)	2940	2810	3000
Ground pressure kg/sq. cm	0.85	0.85	0.72
Fighting weight (kg)	24000	23458	23000
Crew	4 to 5	6	5
Fuel consumption (liters\100 km, on/off road)		200/350	160\300
Fuel capacity (liters)		470 (2 tanks)	500
Hull armor front (mm)	30	20	30
sides (mm)	20	20	16
rear (mm)	20	20	16
Turret armor front (mm)	upper body 10	upper body 10	30
sides (mm)	10	10	16
rear (mm)	10	10	10
Climbing (degrees)	30	30	30
Step (mm)	600	600	750
Fording (mm)	800	1000	1400
Crossing (mm)	2300	2300	2300
Weapons, primary	1 8.8 cm Pak 43/1 (L/71) (40)	1 15 cm sFH 18 (M) (18)	1 10.5 cm leFH 43 (L/35) (60)
secondary	1 MG 34 (loose) (600)		
Notes			

Vehicle designation	leFH 18/1 (Sf) Gw IV b (Sd.Kfz.165/1)	Munitionsträger für Karlgerät	Panzerfähre (Pz.F.)
Ausf.	–	–	–
Type	–	–	–
Manufacturer	Krupp-Grusonwerk AG	Krupp-Grusonwerk AG	Klöckner-Humboldt-Deutz AG
Years built	1942	1941	1942
Information source	Handbook WaA. G 361		

Engine	Maybach HL 66 p		Maybach HL 120 TRM
Cylinders	6 in-line		60-degree V12
Bore x stroke (mm)	105 x 130		105 x 115
Displacement (cc)	6754		11867
Compression ratio	6.7 : 1		6.5 : 1
RPM normal/maximum	3200		2600/3000
Horsepower	180		265/300
Valves	Dropped		Dropped, 1 camshaft per cylinder head
Crankshaft	8 journal bearings		7 roller bearings
Carburetors	2 Solex 40 JFF II		2 Solex 40 JFF II
Firing order	1-5-3-6-2-4		1-12-5-8-3-10-6-7-2-11-4-9
Starter	Bosch BNG 2.5/12		Bosch BNG 4/24
Generator	Bosch RKCK 130/12-825		Bosch GTLN 600/12-1500
Batteries	2 12-volt, 105 Ah		2 12-volt, 105 Ah
Fuel pumps	Pumps		2 mechanical, 1 electric
Coolant	Water		Water

Clutch		F & S La 120/HDA dry 3-plate	
Transmission		ZF SSG 76 Aphon	
Speeds		6 forward, 1 reverse	
Drive wheels		Front	
Axle ratio		1 : 3.23	
Top speed		45 km/hr	
Range on/off road		240/130 km	
Steering		Krupp-Wilson clutch	
Turning circle		5.92 meters	

Springs	Longitudinal quarter-elliptic		Longitudinal quarter-elliptic, 4 trucks
Lubrication		High-pressure	
Brake system		Fried.Krupp AG	
Brake operation		Mechanical	
Brake type		External	
Brake effect on		Drive wheels	
Running gear		Road wheels + return rollers	
Road wheel size		470 x 75-660	
Track base (mm)		2450	
Track length (mm)	2500	3520	3880
Track width (mm)	400	400	400
Links per track	81	99	107
Track type		Kgs 61/400/120	
Ground clearance (mm)		400	
Overall length (mm)	5900	5948	8250
Overall width (mm)	2870	2880	2800
Overall height (mm)	2250	2720	2800
Ground pressure kg/sq. cm	0.73		
Fighting weight (kg)	17000		17000
Crew	5	2	3
Fuel consumption (liters/100 km on/off road)	170/315	200/350	200/350
Fuel capacity (liters)	410	470 (3 tanks)	470 (3 tanks)

Hull armor front (mm)	20		14.5
sides (mm)			14.5
rear (mm)	14.5		14.5
Turret armor front (mm)	20		–
sides (mm)	14,5		–
rear (mm)	14.5		–
Climbing (degrees)	30	30	30
Step (mm)	600	600	600
Fording (mm)	800	1000	floats
Crossing (mm)	2100	2300	2500
Weapons primary	1 10.5 cm leFH 18/(L/28) (60)	none	none
secondary			
Notes			

Bibliography

Willi A. Bölke, *Deutschlands Rüstung im Zweiten Weltkrieg*

Heinz Guderian, *Erinnerungen eines Soldaten*

Fritz Heigl, *Taschenbuch der Tanks*

Robert J. Icks, *Tanks and Armored Vehicles*

P. Kantakoski, *Suomalaiset panssarivaunujoukot*

Janusz Magnuski, *Wozy Bojowe*

F. W. von Mellenthin, *Panzer Battles*

Oskar Munzel, *Die deutschen gepanzerten Truppen bis 1945*

Walther K. Nehring, *Die Geschichte der deutschen Panzerwaffe 1916-1945*

R. M. Ogorkieziez, *Armour*

Werner Oswald, *Kraftfahrzeuge und Panzer der Reichswehr, Wehrmacht und Bundeswehr*

Norbert Schausberger, *Rüstung in Österreich 1938-1945*

H. Scheibert & C. Wagener, *Die deutsche Panzertruppe 1939-1945*

F, M. von Senger und Etterlin, *Die deutschen Panzer 1926-1945*

Walter J. Spielberger, *Die deutschen Panzerkampfwagen III und IV mit ihren Abarten*

Walter J. Spielberger, *Der Panzerkampfwagen IV und seine Abarten 1935-1945*

Walter J. Spielberger & Uwe Feist, *Armor Series* 1-10

Walter J. Spielberger & Uwe Feist, *Panzerkampfwagen IV–Workhorse of the German Panzertruppe*

Walter J. Spielberger, *Profile–Panzerkampfwagen Ausf. F*

Rolf Stoves, *Die 1. Panzer Division*

Abbreviations

a/	
a/A	old type, old version
A (2)	Infantry Dept., War Ministry
A (4)	Field Artillery Dept., War Ministry
A (5)	Foot Artillery Dept., War Ministry
A 7 V	Traffic Dept., War Ministry
AD (2)	General War Dept., Section 2 (Infantry)
AD (4)	General War Dept., Section 4 (Field Artillery)
AD (5)	General War Dept., Section 5 (Foot Artillery)
AHA/Ag K	General War Dept.,
AK	Artillery Design Bureau
AKK	Army Vehicle Column
ALkw	Army Truck
ALZ	Army Truck Convoy
AOK	Army High Command
APK	Artillery Testing Commission
ARW	Eight-wheel vehicle
A-Typen	All-wheel drive
BAK	Anti-Balloon Cannon
Bekraft	Fuel Dept., Field Vehicles
BMW	Bayerische Motoren Werke
Chefkraft	Chief, Field Vehicles
(DB)	Daimler-Benz
DMG	Daimler-Motoren-Gesellschaft
Dtschr. Krprz.	German Crown Prince
E-Fahrgestell	Uniform chassis
E-Pkw	Uniform passenger vehicle
E-Lkw	Uniform freight vehicle
Fa	Field Artillery
FAMO	Fahrzeug- und Motorenbau GmbH
Fgst	Chassis
FF-Kabel	Field phone cable
FH	Field howitzer
FK	Field cannon, field gun
Flak	Anti-aircraft gun
F. T.	Radio/telegraph
Fu	Radio
Fu Ger	Radio set
Fu Spr Ger	Radio speaker set
g	Secret
Gen. St. d. H.	Army General Staff
Gengas	Generator gas
G. I. d. MV.	General Inspection of Military Traffic
g. Kdos.	Secret command material
gp	Armored
g. RS	Secret government material
gl	Off-road capable
GPD	Rifle Testing Commission
Gw	Armed vehicle
(H)	Rear engine
Hanomag	Hannoversche Maschinenbau AG
HK	Halftrack
H.Techn.V.Bl.	Army Technical Instructions
HWA	Army Weapons Office
I. D.	Infantry Division
I. G.	Infantry Gun
In.	Inspection
In. 6	Inspection, Motor Vehicles
Ikraft	Inspection, Field Vehicles
ILuk	Inspection, Air and Ground Vehicles
K	Cannon, gun
KD	Krupp-Daimler
K. D.	Cavalry Division
KdF	Strength Through Joy (Nazi organization)

K. d. K.	Commander, Motorized Troops
K. Flak	Vehicle-mounted anti-aircraft gun
Kfz.	Motor Vehicle
k	small
KM	War Ministry
KP	Limber
(Kp)	Krupp
Kogenluft	Commanding General, Air Forces
Krad	Motorcycle
Kr. Zgm.	Towing Tractor
KS	Fuel injection
Kw	Vehicle or combat vehicle
KrKW	Ambulance
KOM	Motor Bus
KwK	Tank gun
l	Light
L/	Caliber length
le	Light
le FH	Light field howitzer
le FK	Light field gun
l. F. H.	Light field howitzer
le. I. G.	Light infantry gun
le. W. S.	Light Wehrmacht tractor
LHB	Linke-Hoffmann-Busch
l. I. G.	Light infantry gun
Lkw	Truck
LWS	Land-water tractor
m	Medium
MAN	Maschinenfabrik Augsburg-Nürnberg AG
MG	Machine gun
MP	Machine pistol
MTW	Personnel Carrier
Mun.Pz.	Armored ammunition carrier
n	Revolutions per minute
n/A	New type, new version
NAG	Nationale Automobilgesellschaft
(o)	Standard trade type
Ob. d. H.	Commander of the Army
O. H. L.	Supreme Command, Army
O. K. H.	Army High Command
O. K. W.	Wehrmacht High Command
Pak	Antitank gun
P. D.	Panzer Division, Armored Division
Pf	Engineer vehicle
Pkw	Passenger car
Pz. F.	Armored ferry
Pz. Kpfw.	Tank

Pz. Sp. Wg.	Armored recon. car
Pz. Jg.	Panzerjäger
Pz. Bef. Wg.	Armored command vehicle
(R)	Tracked vehicle
R/R	Wheel/track vehicle
(RhB)	Rheinmetall-Borsig
RS	Tracked towing tractor
RSG	Tracked mountain vehicle
RSO	Eastern type tractor
RV	Communications
Sankra	Ambulance
s	Heavy
sFH	Heavy field howitzer
schg.	Rail capable
Schlp.	Tractor
schf.	Amphibious
Sd. Kfz.	Special motor vehicle
Sf	Self-propelled
Sfl.	Self-propelled
S-Typen	Rear-wheel drive (Schell type)
SmK	Armor piercing, small calibre, projectile
SPW	Armored personnel carrier
SSW-Zug	Siemens-Schuckert-Werke train
s. W. s.	Heavy Wehrmacht tractor
StuG	Assault gun
StuK	Assault cannon
StuH	Assault howitzer
Tak	Antitank gun
Takraft	Technical Dept., Inspection, Motor Vehicles
TF	Radio frequency
Tp	Tropical version
Vakraft	Test Dept., Field Vehicles (WWI), Test Dept., Inspection, Motor Vehicles (Reichswehr & Wehrmacht)
ve	Fully grounded
v/max	Top speed, maximum velocity
Vo	Initial velocity
VPK	Vehicle Technical Testing Commission
Vs. Kfz.	Experimental vehicle
VK	Volksketten test vehicle
ZF	Zahnradfabrik Friedrichshafen
ZRW	Ten-wheeled vehicle
Zgkw	Towing tractor
WaPrüf/WaPrw	Weapons Testing Department
Wumba	Weapon and Ammunition Procurement Office
wg	mphibious

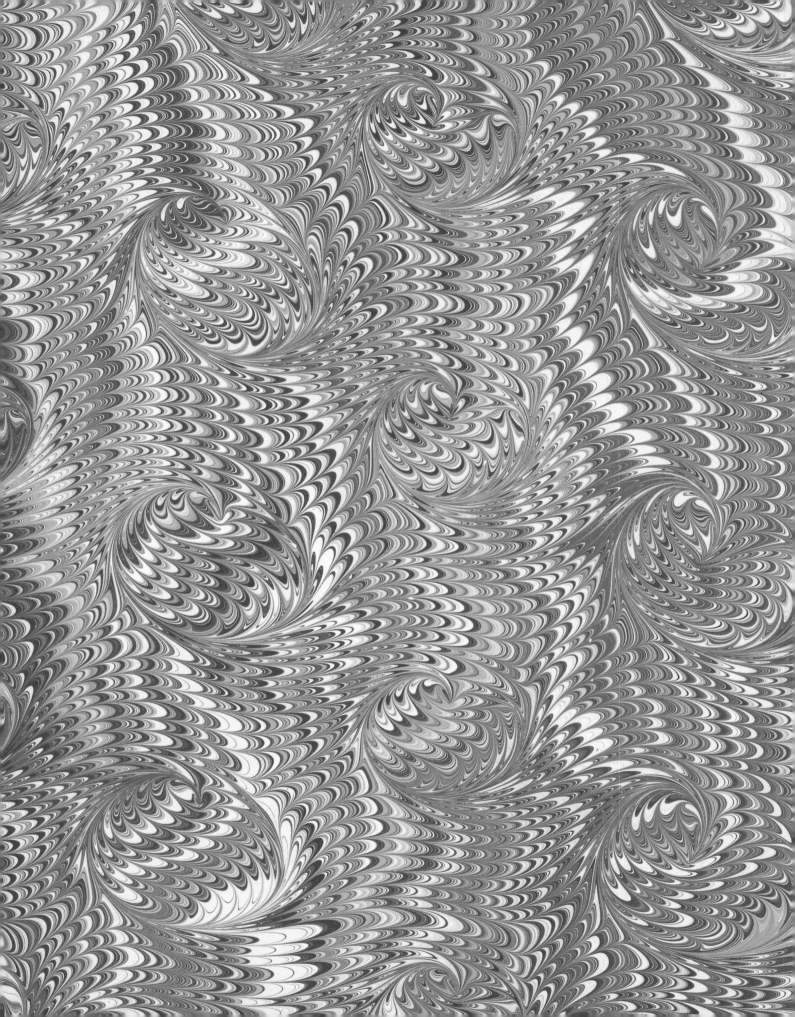